VIRTUAL

GROUP

COACHING

A Research Study

by Pamela R. Van Dyke, Ph.D.

ISBN: 13: 978-1-945216-00-8 (pbk)

This book is

dedicated to my biggest fan

Linda Rea Van Dyke

TABLE OF CONTENTS

LIST OF FIGURES

LIST OF TABLES

ACKNOWLEDGEMENTS

Oran a azu nwa is the African translation for *it takes a village to raise a child* (Clinton, 1994). Although I wasn't raising a child, it did take a village to complete this project. I could have never embarked upon this journey alone much less completed it without the support of several key individuals.

I have been in some form of school most of my life. I consider myself a *life-long* learner. The first people I would like to thank are those people in my life, past and present, that never encouraged or ask me any questions regarding my education or my dissertation journey during the past several years. This lack of engagement from them only deepened my resolve and helped to strengthen my perseverant spirit. I have learned to become very grateful for those individuals past and present, in my life. In contrast, there have been others in my life that have been there for me even when they did not know how to be. Through this long arduous journey they have provided *bread* along the way; sometimes even when they did not know what they were providing to me was some much needed nourishment.

In the summer of 2006, Charlie Seashore became more than just a faculty member to me but a true mentor and coach. He left this world in 2013, the Organizational Development community will be forever changed by the contributions he made.

Supposedly, you only get one mother in this life, but for me I have had the privileged of having two. My mother-in-law, Patricia Smith Fazi, was by far one of my biggest fans while I was struggling through getting a Ph.D. She may not have always understood everything that I was working on or even why I wanted another degree but, she knew enough to know it was important to me and therefore she made it important to her. I only wish she could have witnessed the completion of this project. I will forever be grateful for her unconditional, undying support of me and my educational journey. My biological mother, Lugene Walters, unfortunately was unable to understand any of my journey; but was always there to provide me with the right amount of reality and humor I needed at just the right time. I will forever be grateful to her for the characteristics of hers that I carry with me especially, how to be authentic and to be grateful for whatever circumstances you may find yourself.

Most importantly, I would like to acknowledge my spouse and life-long partner, Linda Rea Van Dyke. There are no words that I can write or say that would adequately capture how I feel about how she has helped me during this journey. She has always championed me in whatever project I was immersed in at the time. She has walked this path with me every step of the way and has done so with a grace that only she could bestow. I am so very grateful and indebted to her.

FOREWORD
BY PETER HAWKINS

"In the world of hyper-change and global inter-dependency, we can no longer afford to evolve Human Consciousness one person at a time."

This was the opening line of a recent key-note address I gave at a coaching conference on the challenges facing coaching in the next thirty years. In this talk I argued that we need to move from individual coaching to group, team and whole system coaching.

Group and Team Coaching have long been neglected aspects of the Coaching world. But in the last few years we have seen an upsurge in interest, new publications, trainings and research (Wageman et a 2008l; Hackman 2011; Hawkins 2011, 2014; Hawkins et al 2014; Thornton 2010 &2014; Britton, J. 2010 &2013; Kets de Vries 2005 & 2011; Clutterbuck 2007). The move from individual to group coaching has been partly driven by the need to coach more people in a cost effective way. However, more crucially there has been a growing recognition that coaching in a group setting can enhance and accelerate individual learning and development.

Pam Van Dyke has made a significant contribution to the research, literature and practice of Group Coaching particularly when working virtually. She defines group coaching as:

> *A horizontal approach to coaching whereby the intervention is delivered to a group of individuals focused on using the group as a vehicle to accomplish their goals and objectives.*

She further defines the approach as:

> *In group coaching, the purpose is to engage each individual on their respective goals by using the vehicle of group process. Leveraging the input of other members in the group, individual awareness can be increased.*

Her research starts out to address the question:

> *It would be natural for one to ask what is it about coaching in a group setting that is different and potentially more powerful than that which occurs in a one-on-one setting.*

This is explored by addressing:

> *"What are the experiences of business professionals in a virtual group coaching process?"*

She begins by quoting one of the founders of Humanistic Psychology in organisations Kurt Lewin:

> *"it is easier to change individuals formed into a group than to change any one of them separately" (Lewin, 1947, p. 344).*

Her research focuses on how you enable virtual group coaching, which has been relatively ignored in the literature. There a few notable exceptions to this including: Britton (2013) who has an interesting chapter 7 in her book on the tools, techniques and design for virtual group coaching; and Goodman and Stewart (2011) who together have provided a useful approach to facilitating virtual action learning groups, which are a widely used variant of group coaching.

Pam Van Dyke's research centres on 21 business people who had taken part in different virtual group coaching between 2001-2010, which had been conducted by four different professionally accredited coaches. Although 18 were based in the USA, one respondent was from Canada and two from Australia.

In her research she discovers that the participants most valued: the time efficient way in which they received help from a diverse variety of peers in addressing their business issues; the personal development that emerged from the challenge, feedback and facilitation they received; as well as the indirect benefits of learning how to work in a virtual group and what they learned by witnessing the facilitation.

She concludes:

There is both an art and a science to creating a virtual presence both during the session as well as in between meetings.

Pam Van Dyke's study has implications for the profession and for the training of coaches. Increasingly Coach training programmes are including modules on group and team coaching, but these are often very limited in time and scope. She points out that very few coaching schools currently provide training in working with virtual coaching and even less the art and science of virtual group coaching. As we accelerate faster and faster into the digital age, coaches will need to learn how to work effectively in both virtual and group environments. Pam Van Dyke has provided us with some very useful findings to help coaches on this exciting journey.

Peter Hawkins

Professor of Leadership Henley Business School, Chairman of Renewal Associates (www.renewalassociates.co.uk) and Author of many books including "Leadership Team Coaching" and "Leadership Team Coaching in Practice."

1

VIRTUAL

GROUP COACHING:

AN INTRODUCTION

Coaching is an emerging and evolving field, complex and dynamic, integrating the ideas, theories, and approaches of many theorists and researchers both past and present. Coaches, for decades, have been sought to help improve performance (Short & Short, 2005). Although athletic coaches initially paved the way (Gallwey, 1976), coaches have been used in a variety of fields for many years to assist individuals to improve in areas such as music, language, and drama, all employed with the express purpose of enhancing performance. Business professionals are no different. They, too, have sought out and hired coaches to help them enhance their performance (Weller & Weller, 2004).

As organizations have become more complex in this global realm, enhancing one's performance and achieving leader effectiveness has become more complicated. One way organizations are choosing to assist in enhancing leader effectiveness is through the intervention of executive coaching (Weller & Weller, 2004). It is a performance strategy that has become more widely accepted and utilized by corporations and as a result has increased the level of interest of researchers (Kampa-Kokesch & Anderson, 2001). Although the literature has grown significantly in the past decade with the growth of the field; there still remain many empirical gaps, one of which is the study of group coaching environments. Much work remains before the field of coaching will be seen as a stand-alone profession.

The first step in enhancing one's performance in any area is to acknowledge and identify the need for improvement. Such self-knowledge can be extremely difficult to come by alone. It is often through the help of others that our insight is increased (Kets de Vries, 2005). Although one-on-one coaching can be very effective, it is often through approaches that utilize group techniques that lead to greater commitment and increased accountability at the individual level (Cohen & Bailey, 1997; Hogg & Tindale, 2003; Kets de Vries, 2005). The group to which an individual belongs is the grounding for his perceptions, feelings, and actions (Lewin, 1945).

Participating in exercises as a group can lead to improvement and results that individuals have difficulty achieving on their own (Kets de Vries, 2005).

Leaders with the inability to acknowledge and address their areas of needed improvement put themselves at risk. "Highly placed managers who are blind to their problems put their effectiveness and their careers at risk" (Kaplan, 1991, p. 3). It is Kaplan's belief that it is not their weaknesses that derailed these executives, but the inability to acknowledge and learn from one's experience that caused the most problems. Developing an accurate self-assessment is one of the most basic challenges for leaders to understand (Kaplan, 1991).

One approach that has been used to help raise awareness in others is the vehicle of *group*. Groups can help individuals get to a deeper, more meaningful level, often more quickly than one-on-one experiences (Lewin, 1945). Whether formally planned or not, groups can be very powerful vehicles for evoking change in others. Formal groups, informal groups, family groups, organizational groups, task groups, survival groups, therapy groups, and so on, can all be used as transformational, effective experiences (Bion, 1961). Being a part of a group gives individuals a sense of being larger, greater, and better than they really are. Group membership is a way of fulfilling our ego ideal (Kets de Vries, 1991). Groups have changed the lives of people and have been an impetus for change in personal and organizational productivity. In contrast, one-on-one interventions do not have the same level of impact (Stober & Grant, 2006).

It is at the intersection of coaching and the group experience that this study sits. This study can be defined as exploring the coaching process with a group of individuals who are being coached by a professional executive coach utilizing the vehicle of *group process* to accomplish the goals and objectives of the individual. Investigating and gaining an understanding of how business professionals experience a *virtual group coaching process* will not only explore insights beneficial to the leadership development and group dynamics areas, but will provide insights into how adults learn in virtual communities. These insights will allow for contribution to the literature in both coaching and group dynamics and as a result, more effective leaders may emerge as a result of this study.

BACKGROUND AND

PURPOSE OF THE STUDY

The first line of Mary Beth O'Neill's book, *Executive Coaching with Backbone and Heart,* reads, "I did not set out to become an executive coach. I evolved into one" (O'Neill, 2000, p. xi). This sentence speaks to how change agents from adult education, business, and management disciplines are declaring an interest in coaching, stepping forward and working as professional coaches (Grant 2003).

Coaching is still in the process of establishing itself from a field of study to a viable discipline with credibility that consists of an effective means for change and growth (Kets de Vries, 2005; Stober & Grant, 2006). "Linking coaching practice with existing, applicable bases of knowledge of science and practice is an important step in enhancing credibility and in shifting from focusing primarily on techniques and skills to a broader and deeper understanding of relevant knowledge in coach education" (Stober & Grant, 2006, p. 1).

At the same time, consumers of coaching services, human resources professionals, and business organizations have grown more sophisticated about coaching services and how they employ coaches for their organizations. These consumers are asking provocative questions ranging from the assessments coaches are administering to the credentials they hold. This was not the case 5 or even 10 years ago (Brock, 2008). Additionally, both private and corporate clients are inquiring more about the return on investment, facts, and data about coaching prior to engaging with coaches. This is forcing a different type of coaching conversation about the effectiveness of coaching (Grant, 2003).

In response to these inquiries, the development of a scientist–practitioner model of coaching as well as an interest in coaching-related research has emerged over the past decade. The number of empirical research articles has increased four-fold since 1993 (Stober & Grant, 2006).

> The first published peer-reviewed paper on coaching was published in 1937. Between 1937 and 1st May 2009 there were a total of 518 published papers. In the 62 years between 1937 and 1999 there were only a total of 93 articles, PhDs and empirical studies published. In contrast, between 2000 and May 2009 there were

a total 425 articles, PhDs and empirical studies published. There have been 156 outcome studies published since 1980; 104 case studies, 36 within-subject studies and 16 between –subject studies. Of the 16 between-subject studies, only 12 were randomized studies. To further move towards a solid evidence-based approach to coaching, more between subject studies, and particularly randomized outcome studies, are needed (Grant, 2009, p. 113).

Although the field has experienced a tremendous increase in empirical data, the research available on group coaching specific to how it has been defined for this study is nonexistent. Literature that does mention the term *group coaching*, when explored in more detail, is not synonymous with this study's focus. The term group coaching, when used in current literature is often used interchangeably with the terms *team* or *peer coaching* (Showers & Joyce, 1996; Goldsmith, Morgan, & Ogg 2004; Kets de Vries, 2005; Barrett, 2006; Appleby & Phillips, 2007; Thorn, McLeod, & Goldsmith, 2007; Brock, 2008). The definitions, when examined further, are describing intact teams or peer related activities in their approach and intervention design.

This underscores that despite the growing interest in coaching in general, the understanding and scope of group coaching for business professionals continues to lack theoretical clarity. The fact that the definitions lack clarity creates confusion among the professionals who are using the terms interchangeably. Additionally, despite frequent references to coaching as a profession, there still exists a lack of agreement on the basic delineations of a true profession among professional coaches. These include barriers to entry, a shared common body of theories and knowledge, formal qualifications at the university level, discipline and meaningful ways to sanction members, a code of ethics and a standard recognized state and national credential or license regulation (Bullock, Stallybrass, & Trombley, 1988; Williams, 1995).

The word *profession* itself comes from the word *profess* and was originally a religious term referring to an acknowledgement or declaration. Learning from three established disciplines of theology, medicine, and law, a profession or discipline should have the following:

- A defined scope stating the profession's purpose and goals;
- Qualifications for education, experience, and professional development;
- A code of professional conduct to guide what should or should not be done under given circumstances;
- Recognized certification that requires maintenance;
- Standards that are consistent with other peer groups (Williams, 1995).

In review of this list, the field of coaching still has some work to do in order to fully establish itself as a profession and a discipline that is recognized both within and outside of coaching circles. Although in some areas a code of conduct, scope and standards for members has been identified, it is not pervasive. There still exists wide variation which allows for variation in services delivered. There have been relatively few empirical studies specific to these areas that have contributed to the field to help provide clarity for coaching practitioners (Natale & Diamante, 2005).

The interest in coaching has increased the publications related to coaching which is helpful overall to increasing the coaching literature base. As more research studies are conducted and more peer-reviewed articles are written, the understanding of the field of coaching has been strengthened. However, there still exists a noticeable gap in the literature related to group coaching.

As a field develops, it should seek to build a solid foundation with empirically validated knowledge, rigorous peer-reviewed publishing process, and an agreed-upon common language (Grant, 2004). The beginning of any new field struggles because there are no agreed upon definitions, practices, or boundaries that exist (Skiffington & Zeus, 2008). It is with this in mind that this study of group coaching has emerged for me, and I look forward to contributing to the body of empirical research.

Significance

Although there exists a void in the literature on group coaching, the efficacy of group coaching as an approach and how it is emerging within the coaching community is a phenomenon currently beginning to be discussed among professionals in coaching circles (http://www.coachfederation.org/research-education/icf-research-portal/ICF). The topic has garnered more interest in recent years due to the interest among both coaches and clients. What happens in small groups has fascinated social psychologists for centuries (LeBon, 1895, Lewin, 1947, Herr, 1998). Small groups have been studied for centuries by many scholars (Watson, 1928; Lewin, 1951; Yalom, 1975; Corey, 1990; Posthuma, 1999; Hogg & Tindale, 2003; Forsyth, 2006). It is an area that in the 21st century is still considered a trend that must not be ignored (Block, 2008). In addition to coaches, small groups are considered a viable intervention technique for organization development (OD) consultants that can have an impact unlike other intervention options (Block, 2008).

The small group is the place where intimacy and the voice of the individual is valued. It is where fear falls away and one can find relatedness with peers. At their very core, small groups are the center of how the world changes. "It is the configuration of a demographic gathering: it reduces the dominance of those who wish to dominate. The world calls for scale and consistency, what makes [the] difference is the small group" (Block, 2008, p.36). "Most things in this world are accomplished by groups rather than by single individuals working alone" (Forsyth, 2006, p. xxii).

> The experience of all is richer than the experience of one. The group as a whole can see further and more truly than its best member. They lay emphasis upon the way in which the group stimulates the individual to do his best, suggests to him lines of thought he might otherwise have missed or rejected and corrects the errors of individual bias. (Watson, 1928, p. 328)

However, current literature is limited in the area of coaches experimenting with utilizing group coaching as a methodology.

Research Question

It would be natural for one to ask what is it about coaching in a group setting that is different and potentially more powerful than that which occurs in a one-on-one setting. Perhaps the difference, in part, is based on the phenomenon described best by Kurt Lewin, who is credited with the observation that "it is easier to change individuals formed into a group than to change any one of them separately" (Lewin, 1947, p. 344). The group member is almost inevitably confronted with pressure from others in the group to look at behavior and to change or alter behaviors and views. Although he or she does not experience the same one-on-one attention in a group as in an individual coaching session, the power of the group dynamic is at times palpable (McGrath, 1984).

Human behavior cannot be studied in isolation because individuals quite often are members of families, friendship cliques, work groups, churches, and other community associations. Groups have a profound impact on individual behavior and shape action, thoughts, and feelings (Forsyth, 2006). There is potency with individuals meeting together and interacting in a supporting way to produce change (Posthuma, 1999). It is what Foulkes (1948) likened to a hall of mirrors in which members serve as objects, both external and projected, that resonate with their inner reality. Groups are at the cornerstone of social interaction. They provide us with a sense of psychological belonging and of being part of something larger than ourselves (Poole, & Hollingshead, 2005).

Researching this phenomenon in more detail would allow me to further explore how the individuals being coached in a group process are impacted. Therefore, it is with scholarly interest and practitioner passion that I have chosen to combine these areas into my dissertation question so I may discover the experiences of business professionals who participate in a virtual group coaching process. When you combine these ideas, a dissertation question emerges:

What are the experiences of business professionals who participate in a virtual group coaching process?

3

OPERATING DEFINITIONS

Although the field of coaching has been established for years, the concepts of team coaching, peer coaching, group coaching, or coaching within a group setting has only emerged since the late 1990s (Sherman & Freas, 2004). Although there is an increasing awareness among coaches of a need to ground their coaching practices in solid theoretical understanding and agreed upon definitions, there exists a "one size fits all" mentality (Grant & Cavanagh, 2004). This one-size-fits-all mentality has slowed down the maturation process for the coaching community both in theory and in practice (Brock, 2008).

The term *group coaching,* when found in literature is most often reflective of a leader working with his/her team, one leader working with an intact team (Showers & Joyce,

1996; Goldsmith, Morgan, & Ogg, 2004; Kets de Vries, 2005; Barrett, 2006; Appleby & Phillips, 2007; Thorn, McLeod, & Goldsmith; 2007, Brock, 2008). These approaches, although beneficial to the client, had more of a top down or *vertical* approach with the emphasis on accomplishing one leader's objective.

In contrast, the approach of this study is based on an equalitarian or *horizontal* approach with business professionals at a comparable vocation level, not related organizationally, who are being coached in a group setting. The individuals are not interrelated by goals or objectives, but all have the express purpose of gaining insight into their individual areas of needed improvement.

The two approaches raise two very important questions for the coaching community; a) are the vertical and horizontal approaches viable methodologies? b) are the vertical and horizontal approaches *credible* coaching methodologies for business professionals? Conducting empirical research would assist in answering these questions and contribute to the coaching field. In order to close the gap that exists in the literature there is much research to be done. The opportunity to forge new pathways and to contribute to new discoveries is a wide open area.

The following terms will be used in this study and their operational definitions are provided here:

Asynchronous Communication: Communication that does not require that all parties be involved at the same time (Jones, 1998).

Client/Coachee: The individual coaching client is someone who wants to reach a higher level of performance, learning, self-awareness or self-development. He or she is not someone who is seeking emotional healing or relief from psychological pain (Hudson, 1999).

Coaching: "A good general definition of coaching sees coaching as a goal-directed, results-oriented, systematic process in which one person facilitates sustained change in another individual or group through fostering the self-directed learning and personal growth of the coachee" (Cavanagh & Grant, 2006, p. 147).

Credential: A coach who has been credentialed has demonstrated he or she meets or exceeds the minimum standards set forth by credentialing bodies (e.g. ICF):

a) attended a formally accredited coach training program.

b) successfully applied coach training and skills with clients (Vilas, 2003).

Business Coaching: Sometimes used interchangeably with executive coaching. Business or corporate coaching is often paid for by the coachee's employer and is done on company time for a period of 6 months, one year, or longer (Skiffington & Zeus, 2008).

Executive Coach: For the purposes of this research and study, *executive coach* is distinguished from *coach* as someone who completed a coaching certification and has or is working towards a recognized coaching credential by a recognized professional coaching association. The executive coach must be versed in the *business* and the skills the leader needs in order to succeed. He or she is someone who is *coaching leaders* in companies or organizations. Executive coaching is distinct from other types of coaching in two ways:

1.) There exists a partnership among the client, coach, and organization.

2.) The individual goals of an executive coaching engagement must always link back and be subordinated to strategic organizational objectives.

What differentiates executive coaching is its dual focus on working one-on-one to develop the executive as a leader while also helping that leader to achieve business results (Kampa-Kokesch & Anderson, 2001; Kilburg, 2007).

Group: Two or more individuals who are connected to one another by a social relationship (Forsyth, 2006).

Group Coaching: A *horizontal* approach to coaching whereby the intervention is delivered to a group of individuals focused on using *the group* as a vehicle to accomplish their goals and objectives. "It is a facilitated group process led by a professional coach and created with the intention of maximizing the combined energy, experience and wisdom of the participants to achieve organizational and/or individual goals" (G. Cockerham, personal communication, July 7, 2008). This term is not to be confused with the terms *team coaching* or *peer coaching* which are distinctively different in approach and scope.

Laser Coaching: One-on-one coaching outside of the virtual group coaching process to address a specific issue or concern, opportunity, or challenge with the clients. It is generally limited to 10–15 minutes (Kilburg, 1996).

Peer Coaching: Peer coaching is a confidential *process* between two or more professional colleagues who are working together to reflect on their current practices and to hold each other accountable. Both act as the coach and the coachee to challenge, refine, expand and build new skills, acting as thinking partners for one another (Thorn, McLeod, & Goldsmith, 2007).

Self-Development: Can be defined as investigating new perspectives, attitudes, and behaviors, and taking steps to evaluate and improve one's own performance (McCall, 1998).

Synchronous Communication: Communication that occurs with all parties at the same time (Jones, 1998).

Team Coaching: The purpose and entry of the coaching engagement is driven by the leader of an intact team or *team lead*. The coach focuses on the goal of the leader not on goals of the individuals. The purpose of the coaching engagement is generally on improving team effectiveness and generally all are working on the same goals and objectives (Showers &

Joyce, 1996; Goldsmith, 2004; Kets de Vries, 2005; Barrett, 2006; Appleby & Phillips, 2007; Thorn, McLeod & Goldsmith, 2007; Brock, 2008; Skiffington & Zeus, 2008). .

Virtual: In its original form, the word was intended to refer to those things that occurred via the computer. However, during the last decade, the term has been used in various ways to denote to things, activities, and organizations that are realized or carried out chiefly in the electronic medium (Jones, 1998; American Heritage Dictionary, 2002).

Virtual Communities: Passage points for collections of common beliefs that unite people together that are physically separated (Stone, 1991).

4

COACHING

APPROACHES

It is important to further distinguish group coaching from team coaching and peer coaching to fully understand the scope of this research. The newness of the term *group coaching* has often times caused confusion among coaching practitioners causing the three terms to be used interchangeably. In dialogue and in literature (Barrett, 2006) the terms are used interchangeably, perpetuating the confusion. This can connote that the terms mean the same thing which, for the purposes of this study, they do not.

The approach of *group coaching* under study is not widely known nor practiced. It remains an open field of exploration and discovery. Because this area is new, it is important to make sure its distinctiveness is clearly outlined at the beginning of this document to ensure the scope is fully understood. The following diagrams provide clarity around the differences that exist between team, peer, and group coaching.

Figure 1. **Team Coaching Approach.**

In Team Coaching the client is the leader of the team. The executive coach contracts with the leader first, then with the team. Can also be viewed as a *vertical approach*

LEADER

| DIRECT REPORT | DIRECT REPORT | DIRECT REPORT | DIRECT REPORT | DIRECT REPORT |

In team coaching the purpose and entry of the coaching engagement is driven by the leader of an intact team or *team lead* (Barrett, 2006; Skiffington & Zeus, 2008). The coach focuses on the goal of the leader, not on the goals of each individual. The purpose of the coaching engagement is generally on improving the effectiveness of the *team* as a whole. It is a *vertical* approach to coaching meaning everything is focused upwards to the leader. The team is focused on working on the same goals and objectives as outlined by the leader of the team. It often involves team building, developing a newly established team and working to increase the productivity of the team overall. Sometimes team coaching can involve the use of peer coaching to help enhance team effectiveness (Showers & Joyce, 1996; Goldsmith, 2004; Kets de Vries, 2005; Barrett, 2006; Appleby & Phillips, 2007; Thorn, McLeod, & Goldsmith, 2007; Brock, 2008; Skiffington & Zeus, 2008).

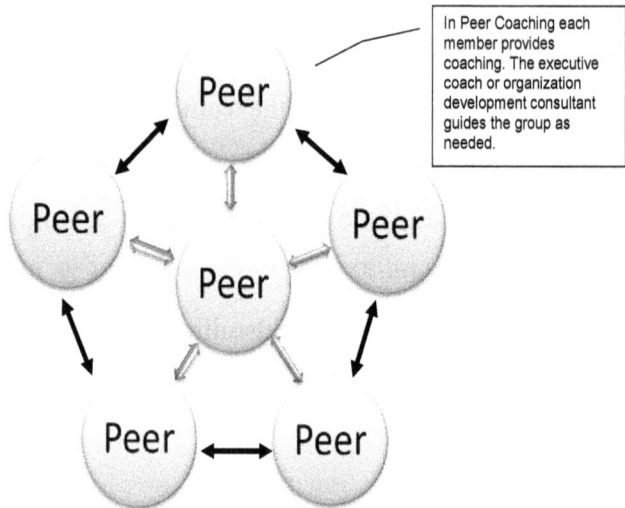

Figure 2. **Peer Coaching Approach**.

Peer coaching was originally developed as a cost-effective way to provide quality coaching to mid-level, high-potential, and emerging leaders (Thorn et al., 2007). In this approach, each participant acts as both the coach, and the coachee. Peers perform the role as thinking partners to their peers. They also help to provide objective support to their peers and hold each other accountable on selected goals. The executive coach, or organization development consultant, acts as a guide in managing the overall project for the organization (Thorn et al., 2007). The emphasis in peer coaching is feedback from each other as it fosters a sense of companionship, friendship, and belonging. It allows others to recognize their strengths and weaknesses safely with the help of their peers. The aspect of non-evaluative feedback is it helps to maintain the enthusiasm and engagement in the process (Skiffington & Zeus, 2008). This approach should not be confused with *group therapy*, which views participants through a medical model while the peer coaching approach views participants as naturally whole, creative and resourceful, and able to generate their own solutions.

Figure 3. **Group Coaching Approach**.

In group coaching, the purpose is to engage each individual on their respective goals by using the *vehicle* of group process. Leveraging the input of other members in the group, individual awareness can be increased (Lewin, 1951; Corey, 1990; Forsyth, 2006). This approach can be referred to as a *horizontal* approach because each individual is at the same level and is not inter-related organizationally. It is one coach working with a group of individuals generally for the same vocation level and focusing on the same improvement area, but not connected by the same leader or organization. In group coaching, the group is used as the vehicle to accomplish awareness and effectiveness within the individual. The coach acts as a facilitator of the group process (McGrath & Argote, 2003).

Situating the Current Study

The field of group coaching is a young field as can be seen in the ICF Global Coaching survey (KPMG, 2008), which estimates there are approximately 30,000 active coaches, most who have been operating less than ten years (Britton, 2010). This dissertation falls within the framework of "professional coaching" while contributing to the understanding of the coaching group processes. The domain of this study in relation to the term *group coaching* is illustrated in Figure 4. This study will add to the qualitative analysis methodology research frameworks in use by other coaching study researchers. It should be noted that the context of professional coaching is central to the outcome of the study, and care should be taken in generalizing the results to other contexts in which the study of group coaching process appears. Central to this study is what experiences business professionals experienced as a result of participating in a group coaching process. The participants who were interviewed in this study were selected at random. Criteria for participation in this study is explained and detailed in Chapter three.

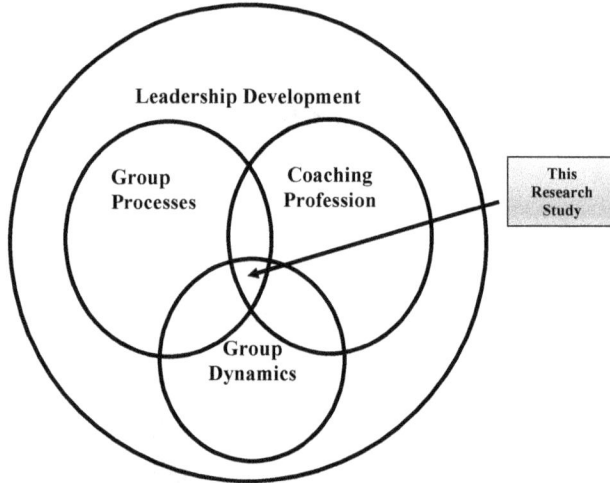

Figure 4. **Situating the Current Study.**

5

LITERATURE REVIEW:

GROUPS

Introduction

In order to understand the context in which this study sits, it is important to understand the two main bodies of knowledge which inform this work. They are coaching and group dynamics. Both have influenced leadership developmental activities in both work and personal behavior (Axelrod, 2005). The developmental and theoretical framework for the study of leaders in a virtual group coaching process is based on the collective contributions of several different theories, models, and approaches both from coaching and group dynamics. This is due in large part to the fact that coaching programs, whether individually or group-based, are an emerging educational and developmental process. They are designed to focus on the performance improvement of business leaders and are grounded in adult learning theory (Hudson, 1999).

As an executive coach who is focused on the development of a leader, one must be grounded in the adult development life cycle in order to be effective (Kress, 2008). The effectiveness of the coaching can be enhanced by the coach's ability to understand and apply a model of adult development that encompasses both career and personal life (Axelrod, 2005). It is therefore imperative for an executive coach to know and understand the various theoretical and developmental contributions that have impacted the emerging field of executive coaching. The field of coaching studies draws from many roots and supports many branches (Brock, 2008).

Most developmental approaches concentrate almost exclusively on the individual leader, ignoring the greater implications of the social context of the group the leader operates within (Day & Halpin, 2004). What behaviors and developmental areas surface in group settings are often times different than in individual settings. Avolio (2005) suggests that in order to develop a leader from all perspectives and within an effective model, consideration should be given to both the dyadic and group levels.

This study will specifically focus on the intersection of coaching and group dynamics by looking into the well-established and researched disciplines such as psychology, sociology, social psychology, and education. Others who have researched these areas (Herr, 1998; Stein, 2003; Barrett, 2006; Brock, 2008) have identified other areas for consideration such as communication studies, self-help movement, social systems theory, athletic motivation, holistic movement, and management and leadership.

These other disciplines have provided a good foundation for advancing group coaching as a field and are inclusive of practice and evidence. This chapter will review the literature related to coaching and group dynamics and propose that extending the study of *group coaching* will yield a greater understanding of the experiences of business professionals in a group process set within the framework of executive coaching.

Group Literature: History

Groups have been considered a cornerstone of human interaction that provides us with a sense of belonging and of being part of something larger than ourselves. They can serve as a testing ground for new ideas, providing us an environment for creativity and growth (Rossman, 1993). Groups challenge, support, and enlighten us in ways not always possible on an individual basis (Bion, 1961).

Groups are described as powerful rather than weak, active rather than passive, fluid rather than static, and catalyzing rather than reifying (Forsyth, 2006). Belonging to a group, regardless of the group's composition or purpose, is among one the most common of human experiences (Rossman, 1993). Human behavior is often reflective of group behavior because we cannot be studied away from our families, friendship circles, or work groups. It is through the membership in groups that we come to refine and identify who we are as individuals. On a practical level, much of the world's work is done by groups (Forsyth, 2006). Therefore it is not difficult to understand why there has been and continues to be so much interest in the study of groups.

Group Dynamics

Gustave Le Bon (1895) was one of the first to study the phenomenon of the small group. He was especially interested in what happens to individuals that are grouped in crowds. He suggested that group behavior is controlled by a group mind such as what occurs in crowds or mobs.

It was soon after Le Bon's work that the formal study of groups began in the 1920s and continued into the 1930s as interest grew in the psychological and social aspects of group life (Cartwright & Zander, 1960). It was in the studies conducted at the Hawthorne plant of the Western Electric Company that researchers began to shift their focus from studying the individual within the group to studying the group as an interactive force (Cartwright & Zander, 1968). This early work contributed to the study of groups and helped form the foundation that would later justify further research on group dynamics.

Group dynamics began as an identifiable field of inquiry in the United States toward the end of the 1930s and is primarily associated with Kurt Lewin who is known to have popularized the term. Lewin (1951) described group dynamics as the way groups and individuals act and react to changing circumstances. He made significant contributions to the field in both research and theory.

The sociopolitical climate during the early 1940s contributed to the interest in the study of group dynamics as a field of inquiry. The American economy was growing rapidly and the idea of mass production was an industrial goal. During the 1940s, traditional research funding, which had been allocated primarily to the natural and biological sciences, was shifting to conducting research on the social problems of the day (Cartwright & Zander, 1960; Rossman, 1993). This shift was seen as a welcomed change and studies began to be conducted at the Iowa Child Welfare Research Station and later at The Research Center for Group Dynamics at MIT (Lewin, 1951). These changes influenced the direction of how groups were studied by both psychologists and sociologists.

Not only did Lewin influence this time period circa World War II, but his impact continued after his death in 1947. He is thought to have revolutionized the study of psychology by empirically showing human behavior was not only a product of one's internal makeup, but by also showing how individuals are greatly affected by the group in which an individual resides (Lewin, 1951; Cartwright & Zander, 1968).

Although Lewin's contributions were significant, group dynamics was not the creation of one person but the development of many over the period of several years and from several different disciplines and professions. Lewin is credited with facilitating a philosophical change in group theory, but he is also accompanied by the work of Homans (1950), Bales (1950), and Thibaut and Kelley (1959). Together these researchers saw the group as a system of interrelated parts, each providing a necessary function, each reliant upon the group's task activity. As the idea of interdependency was redefined, field theory and systems theory emerged as the two major orientations of group dynamics during this time period (Cartwright & Zander, 1968). Group dynamics today has spread far beyond the initial disciplines of psychology and sociology and is now considered to be much more interdisciplinary with branches in other social sciences (Forsyth, 2006).

Lewin's theory of group dynamics has been a major contribution to the social sciences field. His theory outlines that groups are the sum of their parts and presupposes the principle of interactionism. Interactionism assumes that the behavior of the people in the group is determined by the interaction of the person and the environment. The formula used to depict this is B = $f(P,E)$ (Lewin, 1951). "In a group context, this formula implies that the behavior (B) of group members is a function (f) of the interaction of their personal characteristics (P) which include environmental factors (E), and includes features of the group, the group members, and the situation. The whole is greater than the sum of the parts (Forsyth, 2006). Individuals may not like each other in isolation, but when formed into a group setting, they experience powerful feelings of unity and esprit de corps. Individuals who are combined in a group can sometimes accomplish much more as a group than as individuals (Hackman, 1987; Janis, 1983).

Group Cohesion

Although there has been a significant amount of contribution from a variety of researchers, (Lewin, 1947; Homans, 1950; Bion, 1961; Corey & Corey, 1982; Forsyth, 2006), the vocabulary to describe groups and group dynamics varies considerably from one researcher to another. However, most agree once formed, how the group members interact with each other will determine how effective the group will be in accomplishing its tasks.

Forsyth (2006) describes group cohesion as "the strength of the bonds linking individuals to the group, feelings of attraction for specific group members and the group itself, the unity of the group, and the degree to which the group members coordinate their efforts to their goals" (Forsyth, 2006, p. 14). In group coaching, the executive coach utilizes the group to assist clients to achieve their goals. Hence, the group acts as a vehicle for the participants to achieve their goals. Achieving cohesiveness quickly in a group can increase the likelihood of individual's completing the tasks they have identified as needing to complete (Mullen & Copper, 1994). The development of a cohesive group assumes some commonality among the members as it relates to commitment to task completion. In successful group interactions, it is necessary to have a balance between cohesion and task completion (Rossman, 1993).

Group Facilitation

Whereas group dynamics is focused on the study of the individual's behavior in the group, facilitation is more about process and is most often mentioned in conjunction with decision making. There is a distinct difference in presenting information, teaching content, and facilitating process. Facilitation is designed for groups, organizations, networks, and communities. It is focused on *how* you do something rather than the content that is being discussed in the group. The facilitator is facilitating from a neutral place. It involves helping the individuals in the group move from A to B, towards an agreed destination. "Facilitation enables a group of people to achieve their own purpose in their own agreed way" (Hunter, 2007, p. 19). Two primary group processes most often identified with facilitation are problem solving and decision making (Schwartz, 2002).

Facilitation and problem solving directly correlates to my research question in that the business professionals who voluntarily joined the virtual group coaching process did so because they were primarily in search of venue to help them problem solve their business issues. The virtual group coaching process afforded them the opportunity to bring their business challenges and issues, (e.g., staff issues, marketing plans, client conversion problems) to the group for problem-solving solutions. The individuals would *process* these issues as a group virtually thereby helping the business professional who had raised the issue find viable solutions.

Facilitation at its core is concerned with ways to help everyone in the group participate in the decisions that affect them. Facilitation starts from the premise that everyone in the group has an equal say and has a right to participate, the ground is equal, and decision making is for the group to decide. What underlies facilitation is cooperation, consensus, and the collective wisdom of the group and the inherent value of each individual (Hunter, 2007). Facilitation is focused on encouraging individual self-expression and building authenticity with others in the group. One of the key differentiators of facilitation is its focus on consensus decision making also known as collective decision making. This is based on the belief that everyone has the right to be involved in decisions that affect them (Hunter, 2007).

The roots of facilitation can be traced back to the late '80s and '90s with the increase of the total quality movement, the promotion of teamwork in the workplace, and the complexity and advances in technology. Additionally, the contributions of individuals such as Carl Rogers, M. Scott Peck, Chris Argyris, and John Heron have led to facilitation as a new Schwartz profession. The International Association of Facilitators (IAF) was established in 1994 and was instrumental in developing a set of professional facilitator competencies which in turn has strengthened the field, (Schwartz, 2002).

Although group coaching takes place in small groups and relies upon the facilitation competency of a coach there are some main differences between group coaching and group facilitation. One key difference lies in the objectives and goals of the group, as well as the expectation of the participant involved. Coaching groups are individuals brought together specifically for the purposes of learning about themselves; the members are not part of an intact team. The purpose of group coaching is the individual learning of its members (Thornton, 2010). Coaching requires the individual to be involved in setting his or her own goals and to be focused on working towards them in each group coaching meeting, whereas teams that are group facilitated generally have a shared purpose and/or task. There can also be a network of relationships already established. The group's goal is more self-directed resulting in a variety of individual goals with a commitment to aid in each other's learning. This results in a deep, cross-fertilizing learning experience (Thornton, 2010). Group coaching is more focused on individual self-discovery and individual learning, whereas group facilitation is more focused on consensus and group problem solving.

Group Research

Much of the early work on group research was conducted during the 1940s and 1950s and was concerned with why people perform differently in groups as compared to alone (Hogg & Tindale, 2003). By the late 1960s and early 1970s, group research began to lose its central position in the field, much to the dismay of social psychologists in the field. The reasons have been well documented and debated among group researchers (Hogg & Tindale, 2003).

The recent increase in organizational life around the development teams and their effectiveness has created a renewed interest in group research. The areas that have amassed the most attention in the last decade from social psychologists have been on stereotyping and biases associated with intergroup relations (Harrington & Fine, 2000; Hogg & Tindale, 2003). Group phenomena such as group conflict, group composition, and group performance appeared less often in social psychology journals (Hogg & Tindale, 2003). Paradoxically, research *using* small groups is flourishing in specialty areas such as organizational and industrial psychology and management journals (Harrington & Fine, 2000). Organizational psychologists have taken up the study of performance and processes of groups in an effort to increase organizational effectiveness in organization development (OD) circles. Ninety-eight percent of group research articles were published in leading organizational psychology journals during the 1990s (Levine & Moreland, 1990; Hogg & Tindale, 2003).

Researchers (Levine & Moreland, 1990; Moreland, Hogg, & Hains, 1994;

Harrington & Fine, 2000; Hogg & Tindale, 2003) believe that much of the resurgence in group research reflects the increase

in use of groups in organizations. Productivity problems in the United States forced organizations to benchmark other firms in industrial countries such as Japan where the use of groups and teams were more widely used (Krugman, 1991). The United States looked to Japan for more effective models of management and their models of productivity were team and group based. This forced an increase in the use of groups and teams during the late 1980s and early 1990s through which tasks were accomplished in the United States (Cohen & Bailey, 1997).

How groups process information, project development teams, group work, and most recently virtual teaming has become a foundational building block for the way we get things done. This increase has stimulated more research on groups and teams which is now more likely to be done by researchers in professional and management schools rather than researchers in psychology departments (Hogg & Tindale, 2003; Huber & Lewis, 2010). These new conceptual and methodological developments from the different disciplines enable group researchers to approach the research more systemically in rigorous ways which better reflect the realities of today's groups in an organizational context (Hogg & Tindale, 2003; Huber & Lewis, 2010). This new interest in group research also is a reflection of societal developments which have changed the way people live and work in groups. "Societies that were once viewed as mere collections of individuals are gradually being transformed into cultures that embrace a more collectivistic orientation. Corporations continue to evolve into multinational organizations, and with that global perspective has come increased interest in harnessing the power of groups for productive purposes" (Forsyth, 2006, p. xxi).

6

LITERATURE REVIEW: VIRTUAL

Introduction

When I first started on this journey, the *virtual-ness* of our society was just beginning to bourgeon. So much so that, most of my professional colleagues expressed confusion or blank stares when informed of my research focus. I distinctly remember one encounter with two very accomplished coaches at an organizational development conference in 2008 who told me my topic "didn't make sense" and strongly "reconsider" my focus if I wanted to graduate.

When forming my dissertation and research committees the professors involved also questioned my focus area. It took the hiring and firing of several faculty members before I could get the right combination who a) understood the phenomenon I was interested in and b) could support me as I forged a new pathway. Additionally, for several years, I felt alone in the coaching industry when it came to wanting to discuss and research this area of virtual group coaching. I found the idea of relating virtually fascinating and desired to delve deeper. I wanted to research and study in more depth how being virtual could affect the coaching relationship.

This lack of collegial understanding was ironic given that at the time (2008-2010) the majority of coaching schools taught their courses online or virtually. Circa de 2013, while preparing to speak at a conference on the subject of virtual group coaching, I investigated over 23 schools and institutions that did not offer a course of coaching virtually. Interesting.

This lack of awareness contributed to the difficulty of finding current and applicable literature on the subject. Most people could express how "being virtual" was different and was changing the way they interacted with each other but it stopped there. With little to no viable educational materials available, our understanding of all things virtual has not been able to stay current with the ever constant change of technology and its pedagogical implications. Just recently in the past 2 years have I seen more articles and research studies beginning to pepper the literature landscape. It is a topic whose time has come.

Virtual Groups

The advent of the Internet has changed the way we do business and the way we interact with each other. Even how we use the phone and which type of phone, has taken on a whole new meaning. A new workplace has emerged; one in which we have sophisticated the art of communicating with each other without being in the same physical space. Teleconferencing, videoconferencing, instant messaging, webinars, Go-to-Meeting, and Skype in conjunction with the use of email, websites, texting, and the Internet has provided a whole new perspective as a way to understand and get to know each other as people (Brake, 2006). We have become a wireless world, bombarded by technological advances in some instances on a daily, even hourly basis. This intrusion into our psyche allows and *forces us* to connect with each other through a variety of methods (Walther, Bunz, & Bazarova, 2005).

These technology changes have impacted all areas of the business world, including coaching. The ability and in some cases, the preference to conduct coaching with a client virtually, via the Internet, and/or telephonically is increasing. With this increase, it is imperative that research be conducted to show validity in this approach. Therefore, the study conducted examined the experiences of those involved in a virtual group coaching process.

Virtual Communities

Howard Rheingold (1993) first popularized the term *virtual community* by writing about it in his book, *The Virtual Community*. He discussed how virtual communities emerged from the Internet and carried their discussions from the Web into other spaces because of the connections that were made in cyberspace. Since his original version, he has acknowledged that "If I had...learned about social network analysis when I first wrote about cyberspace cultures, I could have saved us all a decade of debate by calling them 'online social networks' instead of 'virtual communities' " (Hrastinski, 2006, p. 13).

A virtual community can be defined as a social network of individuals who are geographically dispersed yet cross geographic boundaries to pursue mutual interests or goals (Rheingold, 1993). People in virtual communities have become very sophisticated and very creative at doing everything that anyone else can do in real life; talk, make plans, laugh, cry, argue, brainstorm, provide emotional support, date, fall in love, play games, produce work, and so on. The only difference is that it is done without a physical body present in the same space. What has been discovered as the virtual communities have evolved during the last decade is that a lot can happen within the boundaries of a virtual community. To the millions who engage in a virtual community, the results have been rewarding and rich and in some cases even addictive (Rheingold, 1993). As more and more organizations and businesses have understood the impact that virtual communities can have on their bottom line, interest in *virtual methodologies* as a way to get business accomplished has increased.

Virtual Teams

Globalization

With the age of globalization and the advances in communication technology, it has become increasingly common for organizations to establish and leverage the use of virtual teams as a way to accomplish work. It is becoming the new way to work. "Suddenly, in a blink of an evolutionary eye, people no longer must be in the same place – *collocated* – in order to work together. Now many people work in virtual teams that transcend distance, time zones, and organizational boundaries" (Lipnack & Stamps, 1997, p. 1.). A virtual team is one where the members are geographically dispersed but linked through various forms of communication such as email, telephone, videoconferencing, and other Internet-based forums (Lipnack & Stamps, 2010). It is "a distributed group of people working together across distances to achieve a common purpose via technology" (Brake, 2006, p. 116). With new technologies emerging every week it has opened up an expansive new fertile territory for working together apart.

Diversity

Although we have the ability to connect via all forms of technology, teams can struggle with keeping the information received as rich as what they receive from face-to-face settings. There can be a reduction in social and contextual clues (Brake, 2006). However, virtual teams can also offer flexibility, responsiveness, and diversity of perspectives in ways that differ from traditional groups.

Companies, that have been successful at creating virtual teams that consistently produced results in their organizations such as Shell Oil, EDS, IBM, Kraft Foods, and Motorola, have learned the importance of creating teams with diversity. Team diversity, which can be defined in many forms, is not just in the area of time and space but also in the area of different disciplines.

Putting people together who approach problem solving differently and who have different styles and perspectives when approaching a challenge can ultimately produce a more well-rounded solution to a problem. The projects assigned to these companies often required a diversity of competencies and perspectives and participants on these teams reported that the ability to work virtually with a variety of communication channels allowed them to be much more effective. "Each team member had areas of competence that were uniquely his or her own, and inevitably, disagreements arose over matters within one person's area of expertise that had repercussions for other team members. But the clash of perspectives produced solutions instead of acrimony (Majchrzak, Malhotra, Stamps, & Lipnack, 2004, p. 133).

In the research that was cited by these authors with these companies the leader of the team was identified as being key to the process. "Much of the work of generating solutions that happened via a variety of virtual methods were carefully orchestrated by the team leader" (Majchrzak, et al., 2004, p. 133). This underscores, yet again, the importance of the facilitator in the process to help teams navigate through these differences. Taking time to understand each other early in the team's development proved to be invaluable to many of these teams.

Productivity

As more teams have become virtual, our understanding of how they work and what makes them work more effectively in their completion of tasks has increased. For example, understanding how best to communicate with each other to get the work done is among one of the most important necessities for virtual teams. Therefore, some teams administer online versions of the Myers-Briggs Type Indicator (MBTI) as a way to help others know their preferences when communicating (Brake, 2006). This information proved very helpful in assisting the team in learning about each other and respecting each other's differences when communicating.

In the limited research that has been conducted on virtual team performance (Brake, 2006; Walther et.al., 2005; Majchrzak et.al., 2004; Jarvenpaa, Knoll, & Leidner. 1998; Lipnack & Stamps, 1997) studies indicate that virtual team performance is closely tied to trust. Teams with low levels of trusts exhibited little initiative and had little social interaction in their messages with each other. Research conducted by Jarvenpaa et al. (1998) indicated that groups with a moderate level of trust were more readily able to identify tasks in need of completion and focus their communication on establishing rules and procedures necessary to complete the assigned project. Additionally, their findings confirmed that in online relationships trust is maintained through consistent performance rather than cognitive or affective perceptions alone (Jarvenpaa et al., 1998). When people do what they say they are going to do, tasks get completed and trust between the members' increases.

In the higher performing virtual teams where tasks were being completed and trust was high, interaction was also high. There were more incidences of instant messaging and more incidences of members exchanging light-hearted communication, i.e., sport scores and levity; (Iacono & Weisband, 1997). In contrast, teams that just focused on work processes that pushed hard to complete the tasks and did so with minimum communication both trust and performance suffered (Jarvenpaa et al., 1998; Iacono & Weisband, 1997). When working on a team, members need to feel the structure of a small group without the constraints that limited them to freely express themselves virtually.

Virtual Trust

Trust in a dyadic relationship emerges from attributes associated with a trustee and a trustor (Mayer, Davis, & Schoorman, 1995). Trust on a collective level that involves trust within groups, teams, or within organizational units is more complicated than dyadic trust because they include multiple trustees; and each of these trustees has different attributes that they are seeking to find within the virtual relationship, (i.e., ability, integrity, and benevolence). Cummins and Bromiley, 1996, defined *collective* trust as a common belief among a *group* of individuals that another individual or group makes a good-faith effort to behave in accordance with the established group commitments and that no one will take advantage of another even if the opportunity presents itself to do so.

Although trust is important in the development of any team it can be pivotal to a virtual team from preventing geographical distance from becoming psychological distance (Snow, Shell, & Davison, 1996). Trust affects other aspects of team functioning that are important such as how quickly the team will form and how effectively the members will work together to achieve results. Therefore, it is imperative for each member of the team to understand going into the experience what the expectations are and what commitments exist for each of them.

Studies that have been conducted on virtual teams (Jarvenpaa et al., 1998; Iacono & Weisband, 1997; Snow et al., 1996) reveal that early on in the development of the team's organization, the establishment of basic principles, rules of engagement, a team charter or a code of ethics is very helpful in assisting the virtual members of the team understand the expectations around being a part of the team. By establishing these guidelines in the beginning members have a better understanding of how to engage with each other and how to be an effective virtual team member. Increasing engagement levels with each other early on in the process helps to increase levels of trust (Lipnack & Stamps, 1997).

What is specific in virtual teams is the presence of electronic forms of communication which introduces more incidences of virtual members having a tendency to be impersonal and task-focused with one another. As tasks get completed, trust increases (Jarvenpaa et al., 1998). In traditional face-to-face relationships Mayer et al., (1995) found that benevolence was more of a predictor of trust, whereas in virtual relationships ability and integrity were strong predictors of trust. Ability referred to a person's skill level and ability to complete the tasks required, whereas integrity referred to the virtual team members' willingness and adherence to the established set principles. In virtual relationships, when one relies upon various forms of electronic communication to accomplish the necessary tasks at hand, being able to predict and rely upon another members' actions is the best aid in helping virtual members' increase trust and grow psychologically close to one another. Stated another way, when one of the team members does what he or she says he/she is going to do, trust happens (Jarvenpaa et al., 1998).

We have always been a transited society, but walk into any office today and you know that things are not as they were a decade ago. Talk with a group of employees today in conversation and many of them will tell you they are working on projects with colleagues who do not work in the same building, same city, or even the same country. If you go one step further and ask them if they have met these individuals, most will tell you they have not and that the only introductions they have had has been via a webcam meeting or another type of virtual medium. What is also important about these employees who are in these virtual relationships is that many of them *prefer* this type of relationship over the face-to-face options. Enabled by the ever changing technology advances, the virtual community is a natural solution for getting things accomplished in our fast-paced, global environment. Clearly, our business landscape has changed (Zofi, 2012).

7

LITERATURE REVIEW:

COACHING

Background

The earliest origins of the word *coaching* was its first use as a noun in the early 1500's to describe a particular kind of wheeled carriage (http://en.wikipedia.org/wiki/Coaching). Hence, the root of the word in its original meaning was used to convey taking someone from the original starting point to a new location (Sztucinski, 2001). The word *coach* was used colloquially in the 1840s at Oxford University to refer to a private tutor who assisted students in preparing for exams. "A thoroughly clever coach was able to advise them from first to last. Under his careful tuition the crew improved steadily" (http://en.wikipedia.org/wiki/Coaching).

Since that time, the word has been commonly used when referring to sports. It is not unreasonable to assume the first mental image when using the term *coach* conjured up for most people, is of a sports coach. In addition to this common image of the sports coach, the word is also used to describe someone who assists others in strengthening their competencies in voice, music, language, drama, and so on (Sztucinski, 2001). These multiple meanings and usages point to the much broader applications the word *coaching* has developed over time.

In 1976, Tim Gallwey published a book entitled *Inner Tennis: Playing the Game*. At the time, it was a small book which was tailored to help tennis players improve their performance at tennis. Since that time, it has crossed many boundaries to teach others the power of leveraging one's *internal* states. His concepts were simple and basic yet profound for those who captured their meaning. Understanding errors in performance usually takes place in one's mind before being expressed in actions (Gallwey, 1976). According to Gallwey, because of the interference that happens from our own minds, we get in touch with very little of our own human potential, preventing us from doing our best (Gallwey, 1976).

Gallwey used the word *inner* to indicate a player's inner state of mind (Gallwey, 1976). These concepts for sports in 1976 were considered significant. Gallwey's approach was different than what the athletic world had experienced to this point. He was suggesting and in some cases beginning to implement something completely new in his approach with athletes than that of his coaching colleagues.

Gallwey claimed if a coach could help a player remove or reduce the internal obstacles he faced, an unexpected ability would flow forth without the need for much technical input from the coach (Gallwey, 1976). Although this approach was met with some resistance from his colleagues, his intentions were not to threaten the other coaches or professionals in the field, but to simply offer a different approach to help athletes learn how to *activate* their own performance by getting in touch with their own internal abilities.

This method reflected much of what Socrates suggested centuries ago, that your role as coach should be to *help* your clients assess something within themselves, not to *tell* them what to do (Altier, 1989; Whitmore, 2003). Gallwey's approach to *helping* the athlete assess his or her own internal strength and abilities was the earliest beginnings of coaching as we know it today. He in a sense had identified the essence of coaching (Whitmore, 2003).

Others who have written and researched in the coaching field (Judge & Cowell, 1997; Machan, 1988; Hudson, 1999; Whitmore, 2003; Silsbee, 2004; Davidson & Gasiorowski, 2006,) have often referenced Gallwey and his earlier description of the coaching relationship in sports and used Gallwey's words as a reference point for the coaching relationship in management circles. His contributions helped to provide a framework for early management consultants just beginning in the field of executive coaching.

Dick Borough, a psychologist, heavily influenced by the athletic field, was the first person to use the actual term *executive coaching* in 1985 (O'Hefferman 1986). He used the term to describe his leadership development activities with executives. Early reviews of this new leadership development technique were being described as a tool that could be effectively administered to both executives and middle managers (Judge & Cowell, 1997). Today, executive coaching is described as a process of learning and behavioral change that is goal oriented and practical (Peterson, 1996).

As the business world evolved, more organizations began to use coaches and coaching because it sounded less threatening than other types of interventions (Tobias, 1996).

Once coaching made it into organizations, the number of executives seeking coaching on their own also increased (Stern, 2004b). This in turn forced consultants and therapists to transform themselves into coaches to meet the demand.

In 1988, a controversial yet significant article appeared in *Forbes* magazine entitled, "Sigmund Freud meets Henry Ford" (Judge & Cowell, 1997). It was a short but thought-provoking article that described a "new kind of *practice* that specialized in helping upwardly mobile managers organize their career climbs" (Machan, 1988, p. 115). Machan described an emergence of management professionals, typically senior level executives, who wanted to talk about work and career problems. The executives wanted something in between management consulting and career advice (Machan, 1988).

This did not fit the traditional "lie-back-on-the couch analysis" (Machan, 1988, p. 1) of their approach, forcing several of these existing clinicians to reinvent the way they were providing services. As a result, they added a management consultant to their group and developed a new kind of consulting service (Machan, 1988). This early approach to providing consulting services offered a hybrid of management consulting and psychotherapy and had become mainstreamed enough in their region that *Forbes* magazine took notice (Judge & Cowell, 1997).

As a new profession, there have been many disciplines that have contributed to the field of coaching and are continuing to influence coaching. From the literature, the disciplines of the social sciences have been the biggest contributors. These include psychology, sociology, linguistics, and anthropology which have all emerged from philosophy since the late 1800s (Berman & Bradt, 2006). Although many disciplines have contributed, psychology has had the greatest influence on coaching to date and many of the tools and models of psychology have been adapted by coaching (Brock, 2008).

There are several uses of the term *coaches* even within the field of coaching. *Personal* or *life coaches* are usually paid for by the coachee and are done on the coachee's time, much like a therapist. A *business, corporate* or *executive coach* is usually paid for by the organization and this type of coaching is often done on company time. There is often an executive sponsor involved who is also considered a client, in addition to the coachee. There are different skills required to coach these two distinctly different types of clients (Stein, 2003).

Definition of Coaching

As each discipline has emerged through the years (psychology, sociology, education, etc.), one of the critical issues that each has faced is that of agreed upon definitions and boundaries. "What is interesting about the beginning of any new profession is that agreed upon definitions, practices and boundaries do not exist. The shared understanding between coaching and its siblings: managing, consulting, leadership and teaching are anything but crisp" (Downey, 2003, p. xii).

The particular struggle that all disciplines face is similar to what coaching is now facing, definitions that in some instances contradict each other and are based on and influenced by the individual practitioner's background, preferences, and training. The professional definitions, boundaries, ethics, and theories can inform coaching's emergence into a profession (Brock, 2008).

Currently, there is not an established definition of coaching that is recognized throughout the coaching field as being the one true definition of coaching. In the literature, the definitions vary with the researcher and as stated before, seem to take on the background and bias of the individual.

Depending on the theoretical orientation of the writer, the definition of coaching can change slightly. For example, the writers below all come from different disciplines which have shaped their definitions of coaching.

John Whitmore (2003), a former race car driver and sports psychologist, describes coaching more in terms of performance and unlocking a person's potential. "It is helping them to learn rather than teaching them" (Whitmore, 1992, p. 8). Fredrick M. Hudson (1999), an organizational development practitioner, takes more of a theme of facilitation rather than instruction approach, which defines coaching as helping the client see options for becoming a more effective human being. "A coach is a person who facilitates experiential learning that results in future oriented abilities….a person who is a trusted role model, adviser, wise person, friend or guide" (Hudson, 1999, p.6). Whereas Druckman and Bjork (1991, p. 61), both educators propose that coaches should be focused on instruction and tutoring. The coach should be about offering hints, feedback, reminders, and redirecting the student's attention to specific tasks in an effort to closely match the expert's performance as closely as possible.

As can be seen, there is still much work to be done attempting to further refine and define coaching. Although there exist common themes, each contributor can have a differing view of coaching. However, most would agree that there are common core themes. These common themes include that coaching is collaborative and egalitarian rather than authoritarian (Stober & Grant, 2006). Coaching should be seen as asking the right questions rather than telling people what to do, that it is not necessarily concerned with subject-matter expertise or advice giving (Stober & Grant, 2006). Throughout the literature one theme is clear: Professional coaching should be linked to a broader body of knowledge and grounded in the appropriate theories and conducted in an informed-practitioner model that is evidenced-based (Stober & Grant, 2006).

8

LITERATURE REVIEW:

COACHING

Psychological Contributions

Unconscious and Conscious

Although Sigmund Freud trained as a medical professional, he developed a method of psychotherapy that became known as psychoanalysis and became the first major force of psychology. It is unusual to go to psychological literature without reading a reference to his work. His contributions to the field of psychology are numerous and distinct. His psychoanalytic interpretation of personal life became a benchmark of interpretation for all of psychotherapy from the 1890s on (Hudson, 1999). "Freud has influenced psychological thinking more than any other individual" (Knowles, 1990, p. 38).

He brought clients to a state of awareness by allowing them to verbalize past experiences through the use of such terms as *unconsciousness,* which is an essential contribution to the practice of executive coaching (Drake, Brennan, & Gortz, 2008). Executive coaches engage in the practice of bringing a client's unconscious to awareness, aiding to the developmental process (Hudson, 1999). His approach was to use spoken words and listening skills that he referred to as the "talking cure" to gather information and influence clients (Freud, 1921). This system and model of personality development was a philosophy of human nature and a method of psychotherapy that many found controversial. Freud stimulated a great deal of controversy, exploration, and further development of personality theory which helped to lay the foundation on which many later systems rest (Corey, 1977).

Individual Psychology

Adler, after having studied with Sigmund Freud for 10 years, left Vienna and founded the Society of Individual Psychology (Hudson, 1999). His focus became individual psychology, emphasizing that behavior is purposeful and goal-directed which correlates with most executive coaching approaches. The Adlerian approach is considered a growth model of development and emphasizes individual responsibility and accountability. Consciousness, not the unconsciousness, is the center of the personality (Corey, 1977). It is on the process of the person finding meaning in life and on becoming *purposeful* that Adlerian psychologists focus.

This approach conforms nicely with the style of most coaches. Adlerian psychology has often been cited as being the most complementary to the field of coaching (Hudson, 1999; Page, 2003; Davidson & Gasiorowski, 2006, Kress, 2008; Drake et al., 2008; Brock, 2008). Adlerian psychology and coaching both share many commonalities, such as looking at people from an optimistic, holistic perspective and attempting to understand people within their current social field and across all domains of life (Page, 2003). Both are most effective when they are goal-oriented and see the process as one education and/or re-education.

Humanistic psychology

Humanistic psychology focuses on the whole person as a conscious agent in which the individual experiences and decides data from several points of view. It is a philosophy of inclusiveness and openness to alternative ideas and solutions (Bohart, 2001). Maslow, Adler, and Rogers are among the psychologists who have influenced coaching by underscoring the humanistic theory of self-actualization. "For coaches, then this foundation assumption of self actualization and its implications guide a major distinction between coaching and related activities such as consulting or mentoring" (Stober, 2006, p. 20).

Abraham Maslow, most known for his hierarchy of needs, was significantly influenced by psychoanalytic theory and studied alongside some of the most well-known psychological contemporaries of his time Alfred Adler, Erich Fromm, and Karen Horney (Page, 2003). He was considered to be the Founder of Humanistic and Transpersonal Psychology and has influenced the field of coaching through his hierarchy of needs theory (Maslow, 1968).

Although he was shaped and influenced by psychoanalysis and felt it provided the best system for analyzing psychopathology and providing psychotherapy, he found it unsatisfactory as a general psychology for all of human thought and behavior. He felt that Freud had answered the need for the pathology that existed and now it was important to address the need for the "healthy half" which is the focus of the coaching (Maslow, 1968, p.5).

Maslow conducted research on people who were free of neurosis or other major personal problems and secondly made the best use of their talents, capabilities and other strengths (Frager & Fadiman, 1987). In developing his theory on self-actualizers, Maslow focused his bias towards active, successful, and intellectual individuals. "Self-actualization is not an absence of problems but a moving from transitional or unreal problems to real problems" (Maslow, 1968, p. 115). It was their strong commitment to their work and a laser focus to their goals that sets these individuals apart in Maslow's mind. His theory is based upon the premise "that man's higher nature rests upon man's lower nature, needing it as a foundation and collapsing without this foundation" (Maslow, 1968, p. 173). There are five basic needs according to Maslow, *physiological, safety, belonging and love, esteem* and *self-actualization.* Maslow's ideas about self-actualization can be helpful in the coaching exchange because it can help stimulate discussion around the client's development and need satisfaction.

Along with Adler, the ideas of Carl Rogers are central to most coaches' philosophy about creating an effective coach-client alliance. Much like Maslow, Rogers focused on the present and the future, not the past. He also felt that growth is possible within all persons and central to one's purpose; it was crucial to Rogers' thought pattern (Frager & Fadiman, 1987). Perhaps Rogers is best known for his client-centered therapy in which he asserted the client, not the therapist, should be the focal point of therapy. Many practitioners in the coaching community have referred to Rogers' work as a grounding theory for their practice (Auerbach, 2001).

A key theme throughout Rogers' material was that he believed well-functioning people are open to new experiences, "not all trees are green, not all men are stern fathers, not all women are rejecting" (Rogers & Dymond, 1954). His contribution to the therapeutic community was that the client was the only one who could heal him / herself if provided an environment free from judgment and one that afforded love and support. His phrase *unconditional positive regard* is still frequently used today in both therapeutic as well as coaching circles (Auerbach, 2001).

Additionally, Rogers emphasized that individuals with high self-esteem rely upon their own personal standards instead of the approval or disapproval of others when evaluating possible courses of action. This focus on well-functioning people with high self-esteem nicely situates Rogers with the coaching field. It is one that supports people in having conscious control of their own lives, accepting themselves with their strengths and weaknesses, "using positive goals for motivation rather than just avoiding distress, and being able to change in important ways throughout their lives" (Auerbach, 2001, p. 23).

Developmental psychology

Robert Kegan, a developmental psychologist, focuses his concepts of development around the idea of consciousness and identifies five levels or "orders of consciousness" that define how a person knows the world or constructs reality (Kegan, 1982). The first three levels are similar to those found in other child and adolescent development texts: *impulsive, egocentric* and *socialized or conformist*. Where Kegan really begins to distinguish himself from others is found more in the last two stages: *autonomous* and *integral.*

According to Kegan, although there are five orders of consciousness, few make it past the third order of consciousness (Kegan, 1982). In one research study Kegan conducted with over 500 professionals, 58% of the sample did not reach the fourth order (Kegan, 1994). It is in transitioning between the third and fourth orders of consciousness in which Kegan has made his greatest contributions to the coaching field, providing the coaching community with the theoretical understanding for transitioning into adult development.

For Kegan, the third order of consciousness, which he believed developed primarily during adolescence, marks the change from the "instrumental mind" to the "socialized mind" (Kegan, 1994). The development of the socialized mind, simply put, allows us to take in the values of others around us.

Ultimately, one of the most significant contributions Kegan makes is in the concept of becoming psychologically empowered to develop new capacities for cognitive constructs as meaning making and self-determination. It is a developmental step that not everyone will take in his or her lifetime (Thomas & Velthouse, 1990). For Kegan, these changes require a shift in our subject-object relationships and a transition from a socialized mind to a self-authorizing mind.

The self-authorizing mind (Kegan, 1994) which is descriptive of the fourth order of consciousness, Kegan referred to as capable of maintaining its own ideologies and principles without relying on outside references. In his material, he correlates this particular stage with challenges around diversity, respecting differences without disgust and distaste (Kegan, 1994). In stage 4, the self constructs a system which generates its own values, and administers itself by regulating and evaluating its values in accordance with its own standard which would then imply that the individual indeed has constructed a standard. According to Kegan, stage 4 self is identified with the system which generates its values and goals (Kegan, 1982).

These stages and how a person does or does not progress into various levels of consciousness have key implications for the executive coach working with leaders and business professionals. It has implications around understanding the level of functioning an individual is able to operate at, potential career advancement or derailment issues. It can also determine how the coach needs to contract with the client or the pace at which the client can go in the coaching relationship (McCall, 1998).

9

LITERATURE REVIEW:
RECAP

Group Dynamics

The field of group dynamics has been around since the early 1930s but was not popularized until the early 1950s through the work of Kurt Lewin (Lewin, 1951). Even though group dynamics has a young history it has stood the test of time and remained an area of interest to practitioners and researchers alike. Understanding the behavior of people in small and large group settings has remained a fascination among psychologists, sociologists, and OD practitioners (Forsyth, 2006; Yalom & Leszcz, 2005). The various intricacies of groups and their impact on individuals who participate in them will likely continue to be researched and written about for decades to come.

With the increase of globalization and big corporate mergers more and more organizations are utilizing groups and in particular virtual groups as a viable way to get work done. They are finding this as a viable methodology to increase performance and engage employees, especially those from the younger generations (Zofi, 2012). Understanding the various intricacies of how groups get work done can be a powerful tool applicable to any business organization today. Organizations are looking for innovative ways to be competitive and maintain financially solvent at the same time. Work flow processes that used to be structured around individual job tasks can now be seen to be more team-based and group focused. Additionally, with the advances in technology, virtual work teams are becoming more and more the norm in the workplace as a means to get work done. (Zofi, 2012; Kozlowski, & Bell, (2003).

Coaching

Coaching has become more widespread in recent years and is becoming recognized as being of value, relevant, and important in business circles. This growth has been noticed world-wide and coaching is now considered an important and sometimes necessary organizational consulting intervention. The demand for executive coaching and coaching related services has particularly increased during the last decade as businesses have become more complex (Stern, 2004a). "Many of the world's most admired corporations, from GE to Goldman Sachs, invest in coaching. Annual spending on coaching in the United States is estimated at roughly $1 billion" (Sherman & Freas, 2004, p. 84).

As of December 2016, ICF one the industry's primary coaching organization's reported, an annual membership that exceeds 20,000 total members in 108 countries. When ICF was founded it was primarily based in North America but by the end of 2011, 48% of their membership were living outside North America. This reflects 801 % increase from 1999 when the organization first began keeping records. In 2011 alone, 6,262 new members joined ICF with an average of 521 new members each month. By December 2011, the number of ICF credentialed coaches holding one of the three ICF credentials Associate Certified Coach, Professional Certified Coach, or Master Certified Coach was at 8,290, larger than any other credentialing system in the world. Currently, membership is growing around the world by an average of 500+ members a month and exceeds 20,000. ICF continues to focus on professional standards while positioning the organization more strategically. There are currently in excess of 120 ICF local chapters in over 50 countries and there are 40 Special Interest Groups (SIGs) related to a plethora of subjects (http://www.coachfederation.org/icf-research/).

Although not as large as ICF, there are other coaching associations located throughout the world whereby individuals can assemble to gain information and education about coaching as well as become a credentialed coach. The International Institute of Coaching (IIC), based in the United Kingdom, is one such organization. IIC was established in 1999 by a group of concerned coaches seeking to help regulate the field of coaching at both the national and international level. It is led by coaches for coaches. IIC's focus is not only on assisting individuals to become credentialed but also on the accreditation of coach training programs. IIC does not publish its membership numbers, however they currently report being in 90 different countries and offering 5 different levels of accreditation (http://internationalinstituteofcoaching.org/what_makes_the_IIC_different.php).

These are but two examples of the coaching foundations and associations that exist. More coaching foundations and associations are emerging each year in an effort to capture the interest and expansion of the field of coaching. Some are affinitive organizations for coaches to assemble, become educated, and share best practices, while others, such as the Institute of Coaching, have a more research and scientific focus. The Institute of Coaching, a professional organization affiliated with the Harvard Medical School, was formed in 2009 to further the intersection between coaching and positive psychology (http://www.instituteofcoaching.org/index.cfm?page=aboutus).

Although these numbers speak to the field of coaching's growth, if training and development professionals within organizations who are seeking leadership development strategies continue to invest in executive coaching, the outcomes of executive coaching must be substantiated by more academic research that is empirical evidenced-based in order to be viewed as a viable business strategy option (Britton, 2010).

Group coaching, in particular, as a viable approach to be used by executive coaches must specifically be empirically researched in order for this area to gain the exposure it needs to be propagated effectively into coach training schools and credentialing programs. Doing so will allow for more coaches to be trained in group coaching techniques thereby helping their clients to experience an approach that could help them in a different way than one-on-one coaching. Research in group coaching will contribute to the body of knowledge that is needed to help the field of coaching become stronger as it seeks to be seen more and more as a discipline.

The research question this study sought to answer, *"What are the experiences of business professionals in a virtual group coaching process?"* brings together two important bodies of knowledge: one that has been thoroughly research and written about group dynamics, and one that we are still discovering coaching. The results of this study will inform both areas as well as highlight natural intersection points.

10

RESEARCH METHODS

INTRODUCTION

This chapter describes the methodological framework and the research plan used to answer the research question:

What are the experiences of business professionals in a virtual group coaching process?

The data collected to answer the research question were primarily gathered from one source: 22 interviews of virtual group coaching participants who had each (with the exception of 2) attended different virtual coaching programs. A description of their experiences was gathered and the results are presented in Chapter 5. This study should be viewed as exploratory rather than comprehensive in that it does not attempt to discover all the experiences the virtual group coaching participants may have experienced during their time during and after the virtual group coaching process. A descriptive, exploratory design is consistent with the current state of inquiry in the emerging field of coaching (Stober, 2005).

Research Design

A review of the literature revealed a void of information related to coaching clients who had experienced a virtual group coaching process. Therefore, my goal was to gain an understanding of the experiences of business professionals who participated in a virtual group coaching process conducted by an executive coach. In an effort to fully understand these unique virtual group coaching processes experienced by these individuals, I elicited individual descriptions and narratives through interviews with these virtual group coaching participants. This method is known as qualitative interviewing. After receiving these interviews, I examined the data, coded, and looked for themes, otherwise known as content thematic analysis (Silverman, 2006).

Qualitative Interviewing

As a researcher, my intention was to gain an understanding of the individual participant's perspective of their unique virtual group coaching experience. In qualitative research, data analysis is a process of making meaning out of interview transcripts and field notes which is what I have attempted to do. It is a creative process, not a mechanical one (Esterberg, 2002). I have worked diligently to convey this information from the individual participant's perspective rather than my own. I have also listened intently to the tone and inflection of the participants' voices since transcripts cannot always adequately convey the information sought regarding perceptions, feelings, or intentions. When appropriate, I asked follow-up or open-ended questions in an effort to gain more insight into the experiences of business professionals in a virtual group coaching process. Rather than simply assuming what they have experienced, I chose to engage with the participants in this way to gain a broader understanding and appreciation of their experiences. As the interviewing experience progressed, my confidence as a researcher increased which affected the amount of information I obtained from the participants. I was able to ask follow-up questions and probe for deeper meaning to questions. As a result, I not only gained more information, I gained more insight into their experiences which ultimately impacted the data I was able to extract from the participants.

By using the qualitative interview approach to gather this information, I, as the researcher, identified the various themes that exist for these individuals and their experiences. This approach also allowed me to document the themes by conducting a thematic analysis, which will pave the way for further study in this area.

Assumptions and Limitations

All research projects should be viewed as contributing to limited bits of knowledge to a particular field of study (Stein, 2003). This project, like most research projects, should be viewed with the full knowledge of its focus as well as its limitations. Care should be taken to understand the methodology used and the way the study was carried out.

This particular study is limited to business professionals who participated in a virtual group coaching process. Because virtual group coaching is a new phenomenon and currently a rarely utilized methodology within the coaching community (Britton, 2010), care should be taken to not interpret the results as exemplary, or even normative, coaching practices. The purpose of this study was to capture the experiences of a sample of virtual group coaching participants so that the results could help to inform the greater coaching community of this particular methodology and to also generate interest among coaching practitioners. Additionally, I hope that by analyzing and writing the results of this study it will encourage other researchers to explore this methodology in greater detail.

This study is based upon the assumption that the first step in improving one's performance in any area is to identify

Dr. Pam Van Dyke

the need for improvement. Gaining such self-knowledge can be extremely difficult to come by alone as it is often through the help of others that our insight is increased and our own self-deception is decreased (McLaughlin & Oksenberg 1988). The ability to be part of a group provides an individual the grounding for his perceptions, feelings, and actions and the ability to change (Lewin, 1945).

11

DATA COLLECTION

Setting and Sample

I started out with a list of 37 potential business professionals to interview. As I went through the list, only 9 of the 37 individuals, (24%), agreed to participate or met criteria for the research study. The initial plan was to identify and interview 18 business professionals who met criteria. This necessitated further recruitment of business professionals who had participated in a virtual group coaching process through networking, posting my requests on Coaching Listservs, and through the use of snowball sampling. My recruitment efforts took an extensive amount of time and prolonged my research study by 3 months.

In the end, my efforts brought forth enough participants which allowed me to meet and exceed my target number of 18 participants. The final number of business professionals in my study was 21 participants. Six participants, (29%), were identified through the use of snowball sampling. Snowball sampling is gathering the sample from a known network where members of the group are asked to identify other members within the group who meet the same criteria, which essentially means asking for referrals (Dattalo, 2008; Fink, 2002). The snowball sampling technique is commonly used when it is difficult to obtain a list of names for sampling purposes or when the population under consideration is hidden due to the sensitivity of the topic under research (Dattalo, 2008; Fink, 2002). In my case, it was difficult to obtain enough names for a robust sampling. Virtual group coaching is a new methodology being used by very few credentialed executive coaches. Identifying participants who met the criteria who were also willing to be interviewed became extremely difficult. However, through the use of several avenues networking, listservs, and snowball sampling I was able to exceed my target of 18.

The sample interviewed for this study was a group of business professionals who had participated in a virtual group coaching process during the time period from 2001 to 2010.

All participants were either referred to the study by a business colleague or an executive coach and agreed to participate voluntarily. All participants were prescreened via a phone call as part of the process and were required to meet the following criteria outlined below prior to acceptance into the research study.

Participants

Participant Criteria

- The virtual group coaching process was conducted and facilitated by a credentialed executive coach or someone with an advanced degree in a related field.

- The virtual group coaching process consisted of business professionals who were not connected internally from the same department or local organization.

- The virtual group coaching process size, where the coaching occurred, ranged from four to eight individuals.

- The virtual group coaching process held to a regular cadence of meetings, (e.g. weekly, bi-weekly, monthly, etc.), and convened at a set time either face-to-face or virtually.

- The virtual group coaching process commitment fell within a range of a minimum of six months to a maximum of 4 years.

The data were collected through a series of consented to and digitally recorded telephone interviews. Redundancy in field research interviews occurs between 12 and 20 participants (French, 1996), therefore my target sample was 18. Through the use of snowball sampling I was able to meet and exceed my target of 18 with a final number of 21 participants.

All participants self-selected into the virtual group coaching process methodology prior to joining the program. I interviewed the 21 individuals utilizing a set of questions approved by my dissertation committee and the Institutional Review Board (IRB) of Fielding Graduate University. Those questions are located in Appendix A. By constructing thematic analysis I was able to categorize the experiences and processes that emerged from the interviews with the help of a qualitative analysis software program entitled NVivo.

Demographics

When I decided to conduct my research on virtual group coaching I understood it would be difficult to locate participants who met the criteria for the study. For those who did agree to participate, 19 of the 21, or 90% of the participants requested a pre-meeting with me to discuss the specifics of the research study. Each participant selected received an email from me which included a *Research Introduction;* a description and purpose of the research study. Upon receipt of that email, I then scheduled a phone conversation with each of those who had specific questions. The purpose of this call was to a) to establish initial contact with each of the selected participants, b) to answer any logistical questions or concerns related to the research study and c) go over the logistics of the interviewing process, (e.g., digitally recording the interview, obtaining the Informed Consent, etc.). The following is a synopsis of what was covered with each participant prior to the actual research interview being conducted:

a) My name and affiliation with Fielding Graduate University

b) The reason and purpose of the study

c) How I received the participant's name (if not known)

d) An overview of the questions

e) The confidentiality of the research study

f) That the session will be digitally tape recorded

After the phone call had taken place, the actual research interview was scheduled at a time convenient for the participant. All 21 participants self-identified as business professionals who had participated in a virtual group coaching process.

This research study was initially limited to participants from the United States but due to the snowballing of participants, 3 other participants outside of the United States were included. Two participants were from Australia and one participant was from Canada. Of the 21 participants, 14 or (67%) were female and 7 or (33%), were male. Seventeen participants self-identified as Caucasian, one African American, and 2 Hispanic. Participants were asked their age range instead of their exact age. Eight of the 21 participants shared their exact age; others chose the age range that reflected their age. Sixty-seven percent of the participants fell into the 46 – 60 age group range. Eighty-one percent of the participants had college degrees with 53% of that 81%

completing master's degrees. A visual display of the demographics can be viewed in Table 1.

Table 1

VIRTUAL GROUP COACHING: RESEARCH PARTICIPANT PROFILE

PARTICIPANT	STATE or COUNTRY	SEX	AGE RANGE	ETHNICITY	EDUCATION
#1	California	Female	46-60	Caucasian	Bachelor of Arts
#2	Washington	Female	46-60	Caucasian	Master of Arts
#3	California	Female	47	Caucasian	Master of Arts
#4	Wisconsin	Female	46-60	Caucasian	Some College
#5	California	Female	61	Caucasian	Master of Arts
#6	Oregon	Male	63	Caucasian	Master of Arts
#7	California	Female	46-60	African American	Bachelor of Arts
#8	Virginia	Male	47	Caucasian	Bachelor of Arts
#9	California	Male	46-60	Caucasian	Master of Arts
#10	Wisconsin	Female	46-60	Caucasian	Some College
#11	Florida	Female	36-45	Caucasian	Master of Arts
#12	Ohio	Male	46-60	Caucasian	Bachelor of Arts
#13	Oregon	Male	36-45	Caucasian	Bachelor of Arts
#14	California	Female	58	Hispanic	J.D.
#15	Georgia	Female	46-60	Caucasian	MBA
#16	New York	Female	46-60	Caucasian	Master of Arts
#17	Canada	Female	46-60	Caucasian	Bachelor of Arts
#18	Australia	Male	64	Caucasian	Some College
#19	Australia	Male	35	Caucasian	Bachelor of Arts
#20	New York	Female	50	Caucasian	Some College
#21	New York	Female	36-45	Hispanic	Bachelor of Arts

Virtual Group Coaching Overview – Participant Profile

Although group coaching is a new coaching methodology I had two participants that had gone through their virtual group coaching process in 2001. This marks the first recorded virtual group coaching participants of record. It was a small group of five women who continued to meet virtually for 3 years, a total of 36 months. Including these two participants, the groups included in the study met from 2001 to 2010 with the majority of the participants attending in 2010. As part of the criteria, each group needed to meet at least 6 months in order to be included in this study. The study groups met over a period from 6 to 48 months, with a mode of 6 months, a mean of 18 months, and a median of 12 months.

The research question was seeking to gather information on the experiences of *business professionals* in a virtual group coaching process. All 21 participants identified as business professionals who had been in their professions for a minimum of 5 years. Financial Advisors and consultants working within the insurance industry made up the largest group, accounting for 11 or (52%) of the participants. Although this 52% identified as *business professionals,* 100%

of this 52% also identified as being in business for themselves; they considered themselves entrepreneurs. The remaining 10 or (48%) were made up of other business executives, executive coaches, an educator, banking director and human resources vice president. I felt that this group of 21 business professionals provided a good mixture of views, perspectives, and experiences for this study. It was important for context to understand what other coaching experiences these individuals had experienced prior to going through this virtual group coaching process. Of the 21 participants, 10 or (48%) had gone through a prior coaching experience, primarily individual coaching.

The virtual part of their experience was very similar. The methodologies employed were the telephone and email. Three or 14% of the participants also used Skype and WebEx methodologies. A more specific breakdown of these specifications can be found in Table 2.

Table 2

VIRTUAL GROUP COACHING OVERVIEW – GROUP PROFILE

PARTICIPANT	VIRTUAL GROUP YEAR	VCG DURATION MONTHS	VOCATION	PRIOR COACHING EXPERIENCE	VIRTUAL METHOD USED
#1	2001	36	Financial Advisor	Yes	Phone Email
#2	2010	12	Financial Advisor	No	Phone Email
#3	2001	36	Educator	No	Phone Email
#4	2004	12	Financial Advisor	No	Phone Email
#5	2002	12	Financial Advisor	Yes	Phone Email
#6	2009	48	Financial Advisor	No	Phone Email
#7	2010	12	Financial Advisor	No	Phone Email
#8	2007	48	Financial Advisor	Yes	Phone Email
#9	2007	36	Business Executive	No	Phone Email Skype
#10	2006	6	Financial Advisor	Yes	Phone Email
#11	2007	12	Executive Coach	No	Phone Email
#12	2007	48	Financial Advisor	No	Phone Email
#13	2010	12	Financial Advisor	No	Phone Email Skype
#14	2008	6	Financial Advisor	Yes	Phone Email Skype
#15	2009	6	Executive Coach	Yes	Phone Email
#16	2008	6	Executive Coach	Yes	Phone Email
#17	2009	6	Executive Coach	Yes	Phone Email
#18	2006	6	Business Executive	Yes	Phone Skype Web-Ex
#19	2010	6	Business Executive	No	Phone Email Skype
#20	2010	6	Banking Director	No	Phone Email
#21	2010	6	HR – VP	Yes	Phone Email

Coaches

As mentioned previously, the coaching field is young by discipline standards and is considered emerging and evolving due to the evolution and fluidity of its standards and practices (Skiffington, & Zeus, 2008; Kilburg, 2007). Therefore, it was imperative for the credibility of this study to make sure that the coaches involved met specific standards and guidelines recognized by a credentialing body such as the International Coaching Federation guidelines. The 21 participants were drawn from the client networks of four different coaches. Each of the four coaches met the following criteria.

- Possessed a bachelor's or master's degree in related field.
- Held an ICF recognized credentialed such as Professional Certified Coach (PCC) or Master Certified Coach (MCC).
- Completed certification(s) in business coaching from an accredited Coach Training school.
- Completed additional training in Group Coaching.
- Considered Executive Coaching their primary focus.

Although making these criteria requirements for each coach further narrowed the recruitment pool, each of the study participants were recipients of similar levels of coaching expertise.

Virtual Groups

As equally important to the study as the participant and executive coach criteria, was the virtual group criterion. As I began my investigation and recruitment efforts I quickly discovered it was very easy to locate one – 12-week group coaching programs in either virtual or face-to-face formats. The gap in coaching literature that exists is *virtual group coaching,* therefore, contributing with a virtual group coaching study of groups that had met for longer than one to three months at a time would be significant contribution to the coaching research community. Additionally, interviewing participants who had spent more time together; i.e. 6 months or longer, created opportunities to hear the experiences from participants who had spent more time together. By establishing this criterion, however, I had once again narrowed down the recruitment pool of participants. Ultimately, the data that I was able to extrapolate came from participants who had been together as a group for a minimum of 6 months to a maximum of 4 years.

There were a total of 21 participants who were interviewed for the study. There were 19 *different* virtual group coaching programs facilitated by 4 different executive coaches. There were 2 groups that had 2 participants from the same virtual group coaching program. In my initial recruiting efforts, I was able to obtain 11 participants. From utilizing the snowballing technique (Browne, 2005) with those 11 participants, I received an additional 12 names for the study which ultimately increased the total number of the study to 21. By utilizing this technique, it also afforded me the opportunity to establish a small network of virtual group coaching colleagues who were interested in this methodology and impending research results. Table 3 provides a breakdown of each of the 21 participants, which executive coach facilitated their virtual group coaching process, which virtual group they were in, and which year they attended.

Table 3: Virtual Group Coaching: Coach and Virtual Group Profile

Participant	Executive Coach	Virtual Group
#1	A	1-2001
#2	A	2-2010
#3	A	3-2001
#4	A	4-2004
#5	A	5-2004
#6	B	6-2009
#7	C	7-2010
#8	B	8-2007
#9	A	9-2007
#10	A	10-2006
#11	A	11-2007
#12	A	11-2007
#13	A	12-2010
#14	A	13-2008
#15	C	14-2009
#16	B	15-2008
#17	D	16-2009
#18	A	17-2009
#19	C	18-2006
#20	D	19-2010
#21	D	19-2010

Interviewing

All of the research interviews were digitally recorded and transcribed. After the initial phone screen process was conducted a formal appointment was scheduled with the participant and the interview was conducted. At the scheduled time, I contacted the participant and before starting the interview, again went over the issue of confidentiality and the importance of speaking openly and honestly to the questions being asked.

Once the interview was completed, the digital file was uploaded and converted into a WAV.file and sent to an external transcriptionist. All files were transcribed and returned to me within 2 to 3 days of being sent. Working with an external transcriptionist afforded me the opportunity to fully focus on facilitating the phone interview session. Transcriptions did however, capture all the words used. For example, it is common for people to use the words, "uh-huh," "um" and "hmm" when starting a sentence or when thinking about a response. Capturing all of these words helped me to remember when the participant seemed to struggle for a response, or had a particular feeling or reaction about a response. It is impossible to capture all of the pauses, overlaps, and vocal intonations. However, I was able to make some notes which I was able to integrate into the transcribed reports that were ultimately factored into my data analysis. Transcribing is in itself an interpretive activity (Esterberg, 2002), which is why I carefully went over each transcription and made corrections before any analysis was begun. This process allowed me the opportunity to further inform myself on the contents of each interview.

All of the phone calls were conducted without technical difficulties, no files were corrupted, and no transcripts were lost. All data have been stored and archived as outlined per IRB guidelines in two different places. The average interview lasted approximately 35-40 minutes.

Data Analysis

The principal way of answering my research question about the experiences of business professionals in a virtual group coaching process was by conducting participant interviews. I used content analysis to look for themes and patterns in the interview data. Content analysis is a technique that examines information or content by creating a system with certain words or themes in the material (Neuman, 2003).

Initially, I read through each of the transcripts twice to acquaint myself with the data. I made notations about my initial impressions in the margins. It was not until after I had read through each transcript a couple times that I began to use my qualitative software program, Nvivo. I transferred each of my transcriptions into Nvivo and began the early stages of manipulating the data into the first round of categories. Taking the advice of Denzin, (1989), I worked hard to view working with the data as a creative process and not a mechanical one. As I read over each report repeatedly, I began to see myself as a researcher/detective seeking to make meaning out of the qualitative data and to ultimately uncover the experiences of these business professionals (Esterberg, 2002). In addition to loading the data into the qualitative software program, I also converted each file into an MP3 file so I could listen to each recording while driving. My intent was to *saturate my memory* and thoughts with the data from my research study (Esterberg, 2002).

Coding

The use of my qualitative software program, Nvivo, assisted me with beginning the early stages of organizing the data. As I read through the various transcripts I began to generate categories that seemed reflective of the information I was reading. This to me was an interpretive and iterative process. "How we code it depends on our theoretical assumptions and the research interests we bring to the project" (Weiss, 1994, p. 155). Before I began I knew certain categories would emerge simply from having gone through the process of interviewing these 21 business professionals. I had already felt somewhat indoctrinated into their experiences and as a result, I started with a few preliminary categories before reading the interviews. "Some coding categories we bring to our studies before ever knowing what the interviews will produce" (Weiss, 1994, p. 155). My initial coding scheme was quite exhaustive and included several subcategories. It took several iterations with the data to begin narrowing down the coding scheme into a manageable, workable list that was accurate and reflective of the major categories, and which also directly addressed my research question. It took me several attempts before I realized that I did not need to make sense of every sentence or every utterance. Instead, I had to ask myself what most directly answers my research question and what will be of interest to the scholarly community (Weiss, 1994).

Through this iterative process some major themes began to emerge, which I was able to capture by using the qualitative software. I then began to review the data an additional time through the lens of these major themes. This process allowed me to focus specifically on the data and how they correlated to these major themes. I looked for new information or data that did not fit into these major themes in an effort to make sure I had captured all the data appropriately.

Initially, I reviewed the data vertically, meaning I took each participant's transcript and read it from top to bottom, reviewing it thoroughly. I then took a horizontal approach which entailed taking each question asked of each of the participants and reviewing the data from question to question, participant to participant. This approach allowed me the opportunity to become very familiar with my data, and as a result, I made many changes to my coding scheme over the course of several weeks. I then, took an affinity approach to the data and categories began to emerge. At the end of this process, I grouped major categories and subcategories together. For example, "business focused" and "business challenges" ultimately rolled up into a larger category entitled "Business Education". The final result from this study was 5 major categories and 23 subcategories.

Intercoder Reliability

After revising and ultimately deciding on my coding scheme which is also called a *data or custom dictionary* (Neuendorf, 2002), I then grouped the data into the various dimensions. Given that the goal of content analysis is to identify and record relatively objective analysis, I sought the assistance of my student reader for an objective view of the data. I provided my student reader a copy of the data dictionary as well as copies of three transcripts to review for reliability of my coding. I discussed the data dictionary with my student reader and answered any questions regarding the instrument.

The student reader took the transcripts, reviewed them, and provided feedback on how she would have coded them. I then integrated and analyzed her coding of the transcripts in comparison with my own using the same interviews to ensure the reliability of the coding process. My student reader provided feedback on the areas of agreement and areas where she viewed the data differently. Information on calculating the percent agreement where the comparisons were made to the information in the transcripts is found in Neuendorf (2002).

I provided my student reader three randomly selected transcripts which included three different lengths in an effort to provide a random sample. The transcripts represented Participant's #7, #9, and #18. On the interview with Participant #7 we agreed 93%, on the interview with Participant #9 we agreed 86%, and on the interview with Participant #18 we agreed 79%. We discussed the areas of disagreement and, based upon that discussion, those insights were integrated into my coding scheme as a result. The inter-rater reliability between me and the student reader was 86%. Inter-rater reliability is an important part of the research process. The standard measure of research quality and an acceptable level of agreement are between 80-90 % (Kolbe and Burnett, 1991). Given that the inter-rater percent fell within this range, I felt confident moving forward.

Researcher Subjectivity

Through the reading of multiple qualitative analysis literature I was made aware of the importance of being neutral and unbiased during the course of my research study (Neuendorf, 2002; Esterberg, 2002; Weiss, 1994). However, I do not believe it is possible to be completely neutral and unbiased throughout the process. What I do think is important is to make transparent our biases and our intentions as a researcher. During the process, I believe I remained in a state of constant reflection and attempted to examine my own feelings, assumptions, motives, and biases as I prepared the interview instrument, interacted with the coaching participants in gathering the data, and ultimately in the analyzing of the data.

Although my efforts were quite sincere and the gentle nudging of my faculty ever present, I realized it was virtually impossible to remain completely neutral in my interpretation of the data, especially given my own involvement in the coaching community. In relation to this study, I consider myself a coach. My knowledge and experience within the coaching community and in particular of the coaching process, ultimately I believe was beneficial in helping me see the experiences of others in a virtual group coaching process from the eyes of the professional coaching community. This knowledge ultimately helped in conducting and analyzing the interviews of the participants.

In collecting the interview data, I followed the interview protocol but I struggled to keep my demeanor to that of a researcher and not that of a coach. At times I did used my coaching skills to help the participants go deeper in thinking more broadly or more in depth about their responses. In doing so, I believe in some instances the result may have helped some participants gain a deeper understanding of their own experiences. In addition to researcher subjectivity, there are some other limitations to my study.

12

CONCLUSION

Two words that have increased in value to me during the past several months have been *research* and *researcher*. Going through a very disciplined process of a research project has taught me not only a lot about the importance of the process but also a lot about myself. Most especially, I have learned the importance of following a rigorous step-by-step process in order to answer a research question thoroughly. The new yet burgeoning field of coaching deserves such rigor. This research project that I designed and embarked upon followed rigorous steps that would be accepted by both the research community and the coaching community.

These steps included establishing a clear understanding of the research design so that the qualitative interviewing process was correctly situated and extrapolated the experiences from the 21 business professionals selected for this study. Each research participant was asked a series of questions using an interview tool approved by the Institutional Review Board (IRB) of Fielding Graduate University. The same steps were followed with each of the research participants to ensure standardization and consistency in the process as well as in the data extraction. This consistency with each participant strengthened the process and helped to provide a large amount of research data for this study. All in all over 300 pages of data were transcribed for this research effort.

The demographics of the participant data were organized in a series of Tables (see Tables 1 – 3) which provided a clear representation of not only each of the 21 participants but of the research participants collectively. In the process of doing this, it further helped to identify additional relationships that existed which had implications for this research study as well as other studies which may follow. Working with the data in a variety of ways helped me as a researcher to understand the data and also to view the data from different perspectives. By going through this disciplined process, the analysis of the data was strengthened.

A final step in the process was coding the data which required that a researcher be very familiar with the data but also be able to *see* the data collectively as well as in its various components. This required working with the data over several months before I felt adequately prepared to effectively code the data. Using thematic analysis, the data went through several iterations before a final coding scheme was established. It is my hope that by following this step-by-step research process it will contribute significantly to the coaching research community.

So, what were the findings found from the data? What themes emerged from the data that will inform how coaches coach? What if any, implications do the data reveal for coaches who desire to effectively conduct group coaching virtually and face-to-face?

NOW WHAT?

The findings were both provocative and insightful for the coaching community. From the data a model of Virtual Group Coaching emerged and can be found in the companion to this book entitled:

The PERFORM Model of Virtual Group Coaching.
If you are interested in being contacted when this book is published in the Fall of 2016 please contact me at drpam@teamandgroupcoach.com .

An exhaustive list of references and sources can be found on the following pages. These references and sources were used to inform this work. I am most grateful for the work that has come before me. I am looking forward to contributing to this very important conversation.

Keep Learning!

Intentionally Left Blank

BIBLIOGRAPHY

Altier, W. (1989). The executive coach. *Executive Excellence,* 6 (10), 11-12.

Altman, I., & Taylor, D., (1973). *Social Penetration: The Development of Interpersonal Relationships.* NewYork: Holt, Rinehart and Winston

American heritage dictionary, (4th ed.). (2002). Boston, MA: Houghton Mifflin.

Appleby, C., & Phillips, C. (2007, October). Team coaching: A systems approach to team development. Seminar conducted at the Organizational Development National Conference, Baltimore, Maryland.

Auerbach, J. (2001). *Personal and executive coaching: The complete guide for mental health professionals.* Ventura, CA: Executive College Press.

Avolio, B.J. (2005). *Leadership development in balance: Made/born.* Mawah, NJ.: Lawrence Erlbaum.

Axelrod, S. (2005). Executive growth along the adult development curve. *Consulting Psychology Journal: Practice and Research, 57, 118-125.*

Bales, R. (1950). Interaction process analysis. In E. P. Hollander & R.G. Hunt (Eds.), *Current perspectives in social psychology.* (pp. 386-393). NY: Oxford University Press.

Barrett, P.T. (2006). The effects of group coaching on executive health and team effectiveness. *Dissertations Abstracts International* (3227469).

Bednar, R; & Kaul, T. (1979). Experiential group research: What never happened. *Journal of Applied Behavioral Science, 15,* 311-319.

Berman, W.; & Bradt, G. (2006). Executive coaching and consulting: "Different strokes for different folks". *Professional Psychology: Research and Practice, 37(3), 244-253.*

Bion, W. (1961). *Experience in groups.* NY: Brunner-Routledge

Block, P. (2008). Nothing is next. *OD for the 21ˢᵗ Century: Trends we must not ignore, 140 (4),* 35-37.

Bohart, A. C. (2001). Humanistic psychology and positive psychology. *American Psychologist,* 56(1), 81–82, 89–90.

Booth, W.C., Colomb, G.C., & Williams, J.M. (2008). *The craft of research,* (3ʳᵈ ed.). Chicago, Il: The University of Chicago Press.

Boyatzis, R. (1982). *The competent manager: A model for effective performance.* NY: John Wiley & Sons.

Bradberry, T.; & Greaves, J. (2005). *The Emotional intelligence quick book.* NY: Simon & Schuster.

Brake, T. (2006). Leading global virtual teams. *Industrial and Commercial Training,* 38, (3), 116-121.

Britton, J. (2010). *Effective group coaching: Tried and tested tools and resources for optimum group coaching results.* Mississauga: Wiley and Sons.

Brock, V. (2008). *Grounded theory of the roots and emergence of coaching.* Unpublished doctoral dissertation, International University of Professional Studies, Maui, Hawaii.

Browne, K. (2005). Snowball sampling: Using social networks to research non-heterosexual women. *International Journal of Social Research Methodology,* 8, 47-60.

Bullock, A., Stallybrass, O.; & Trombley, S. (Eds.). (1988). *The Fontana dictionary of modern thought.* London, UK: Fontana Press.

Cairo, P., Dotlich, D.; & Rhinesmith, S. (2005). The unnatural leader. *T&D, 59*(3), 27-30.

Carey, B. (2001, June 18). Mentors of the mind. *Los Angeles Times,* Health Section, p. 1.

Cartwright, D. (2008). Achieving change in people: Some applications of group dynamics theory. *Group*

Facilitation: A Research and Applications Journal, 9, 59- 65.

Cartwright, D.; & Zander, A. (1960). Group cohesiveness: Introduction. In D. Cartwright & A. Zander (Eds.), *Group dynamics research and theory, 2nd ed., (pp. 69-* 94). NY: Harper & Row.

Cartwright, D.; & Zander, A. (1968). *Group dynamics: Research and theory, (3rd ed.).* NY: Harper & Row.

Cattell, R. (1948). Concepts and methods in the measurement of group syntality. *Psychological Review, 55,* 48-63.

Cavanagh, M.J.; & Grant, A.M. (2006). Coaching psychology and the scientist-practitioner model. In D.A. Lane & S. Corrie (Eds.), *The modern scientist-practitioner: A guide to practice in psychology* (pp. 146-157). London, UK: Routledge Press.

Church, A. (1997). Managerial self-awareness in high performing individuals in organizations. *Journal of Applied Psychology, 82* (2), 281-292.

Church, A. (1998, Winter). Personality: It's not just for therapists anymore. *Performance in Practice,* pp. 3-4.

Church A.; & Waclawski, J. (1998). The relationship between individual personality orientation and executive leadership behavior. *Journal of Occupational & Organizational Psychology, 71,* 99-125.

Church, A., & Waclawski, J., (1999). Influence behaviors and managerial effectiveness in lateral relations. *Human Resource Development Quarterly, 10* (1), 3-34.

Cohen, S., & Bailey, D. (1997). What makes teams work: Group effectiveness research from the shop floor to the executive suite. *Journal of Management, 23,* 239-290.

Coleman, A., & Geller, M. (1985). *Group relations reader 2.* Jupiter, Fl: A.K. Rice Institute.

Cooley, C. (1909). *Social organization.* NY: Scribner.

Corey, G. (1977). *Theory and practice of counseling and psychotherapy* (2nd ed). Monterey, CA: Brooks/Cole.

Corey, G. & Corey, M. (1982). Groups: Process and practice (2nd ed.). Monterey, CA: Brooks/Cole.

Corey, G. (1990). Theory and practice of group counseling (3rd ed.). Monterey: Brook/Cole.

Cummins, L.L., & Bromiley, P. (1996). The Organizational Trust Inventory (OTI): Development and validation. In R.M. Kramer and T.R. Tyler (eds.), *Trust in organizations: Frontiers of theory and research,* (pp. 302-330). Thousand Oaks, CA: Sage Publications.

Dattalo, P. (2008). *Determining sample size: Balancing power, precision, and practicality.* New Your, NY: Oxford University Press.

Davidson, M., & Gasiorowski, F. (2006). Coaching and its use by counseling professionals. *The Journal of Individual Psychology*,62 (2), 188-201.

Day, D.V. (2000). Growing leaders for tomorrow: An introduction. In D. Day, S. Zaccaro, & S. Halpin (Eds.), *Leader development for transforming organizations: Growing leaders for tomorrow* (pp. 3-23). Mawah, NJ.: Lawrence Erlbaum.

Day, D. V., & Halpin, S. M. (2004). Growing leaders for tomorrow: An introduction. In D. V. Day,

S. J. Zacarro, & S. M. Halpin (Eds.), *Leader development for transforming organizations: Growing leaders for tomorrow* (pp. 3-22). Mahwah, NJ: Erlbaum.

Denzin, N. (1989). *The research act* (3rd ed.). Englewood Cliffs, NJ: Prentice Hall.

Denzin, N.K., Lincoln, Y.S. (Eds.). (2003). *The Landscape of qualitative research: Theories and issues.* Thousand Oaks, CA: Sage Publications.

Diedrich, R. (2001). Lessons learned in – and guidelines for – coaching executive teams. *Consulting Psychology Journal: Practice and Research, 53* (4), 238-239.

Downey, M. (2003). *Effective coaching: Lessons from the coaches' coach* (2nd ed.). Mason, OH: Thomson Business and Professional Publishing.

Drake, D., Brennan, D., & Gortz, K. (2008). *The philosophy and practice of executive coaching: Insights and issues for a new era.* Hoboken, NJ: John Wiley & Sons.

Druckman, D., & Bjork, R.A. (1991). *In the mind's eye: Enhancing human performance.* Washington, DC: National Academy Press.

Ducharme, M., (2004). The cognitive-behavioral approach to executive coaching. *Consulting Psychology Journal: Practice and Research, 56(4), 214-224.*

Durkheim, E. (1966). *Suicide.* New York, NY: Free Press. (Original work published in 1897).

Esterberg, K.G. (2002). *Qualitative methods in social research.* Boston, MA: McGraw-Hill.

Filipczak, B. (1998). The executive coach: Helper or healer? *Training*, 35(3), 30-36.

Fink, A. (2002). *How to sample in surveys.* Thousand Oaks, CA: Sage Publications.

Foulkes, S. (1948). *Introduction to group psychotherapy: Studies in the social integration of individuals and groups.* London: Heinemann.

Forsyth, D. (2006). *Introduction to group dynamics.* United States: Thomson Wadsworth Publishing.

Frager, R. & Fadiman, J. (1987). *Personality and personal growth*. London: Pearson Publishing.

French, K.L. (1996). *The mentee's perspective: Understanding mentoring relationships through narrative*. Doctoral dissertation, The Fielding Institute, Santa Barbara, CA.

Freud, S. (1921). Group psychology and the analysis of the ego. In R. Hutchins (Ed.), *Great Books of the western world: Freud* (pp. 664-696). New York, NY: W.W. Norton & Company, Inc.

Gallwey, T. (1976). *Inner tennis: Playing the game*. New York, NY: Random House.

Goldsmith, M., Morgan, H., & Ogg, A. (Eds.). (2004). *Leading organizational learning: Harnessing the power of knowledge*. San Francisco, CA: Jossey-Bass.

Goleman, D. (1998). *Emotional intelligence*. New York, NY: Bantam Books.

Goodstone, M., & Diamante, T. (1998). Organizational use of therapeutic change: Strengthening multisource feedback systems through interdisciplinary coaching. *Consulting Psychology Journal: Practice and Research, 50*, (3), 152-163.

Grant, A. (2003, November 12). *Keeping up with the cheese! Research*

Grant, A. (2004). Keeping up with the cheese! Research as a foundation for professional coaching of the future. In I.F. Stein & L.A. Belsten (Eds.), *Proceedings of the first ICF coaching research symposium* (pp. 1-19).

Grant, A., & Cavanagh, M.J., (2004). Toward a profession of coaching: Sixty-five years of progress and challenges for the future. *International Journal of Evidence Based Coaching and Mentoring* 2 (1) pp. 1-16.

Grant, A. (2009). *Workplace, executive and life coaching: An annotated bibliography from the behavioral science and business literature (May 2009).* Coaching Psychology Unit, University of Sydney, Australia.

Goleman, D. (1998). *Working with emotional intelligence.* New York: Bantam Books.

Goodstone, M., & Diamante, T. (1998). Organizational use of therapeutic change: Strengthening multisource feedback systems through interdisciplinary coaching. *Consulting Psychology Journal: Practice and Research, 50* (3), 152-163.

Hackman, J.R. (1987). The design of work teams. In J.W. Lorsch (Ed.), *Handbook of organizational behavior* (pp. 315-342). Upper Saddle River, NJ: Prentice Hall.

Hall, D., Otazo, K., & Hollenbeck, G. (1999 Winter). Behind closed doors: What really happens in Executive Coaching. *Organizational Dynamics, 27 (3), 39-53.*

Harrington, B. & Fine, G. (2000). Opening the "Black Box": Small groups and twenty-first-century sociology. *Social Psychology Quarterly,* 63 (4), 312-323.

Harris, M. (1999). Practice network: Look, it's an I-O psychologist...No, it's a trainer....No, it's an executive coach. *The Industrial-Organizational Psychologist, 36* (3), 38-42.

Hare, P.A. (2003). Roles, relationships, and groups in organizations: Some conclusions and recommendations. *Small Group Research, 34*(2), 123-154.

Hargrove, R. (2003). *Masterful coaching.* San Francisco, CA: Jossey-Bass/Pfeiffer.

Haudan, J. (2008). *The Art of engagement.* New York, NY: McGraw-Hill.

Heames, J. & Harvey, M. (2006). The evolution of the concept of the "executive" from the 20th century manager to the 21st century global leader. *Journal of Leadership and Organizational Studies, 13*(2), 29-41.

Herr, J. (1998). Group-As-A-Whole-Esteem: Stories and reflection from experienced group facilitators. *Dissertations Abstracts International* (9908019).

Heffernan, P. Silicon Valley's Success Coach. Santa Clara County Business, April 1996.

Hogg, M. & Hains, S. (1994). Back to the future: Social psychology research on groups. *Journal of Experimental Social Psychology, 30,* (6), 527-555.

Hogg, M. & Tindale, S. (2003). *Blackwell handbook of social psychology: Group processes.* Malden, MA: Blackwell.

Homans, G. (1950). *The human group.* New York, NY: Harcourt Brace Jovanovich.

Hrastinski, S. (2006). The relationship between adopting a synchronous medium and participation in online group work: An explorative study. *Interactive Learning Environments,* 14(2), 137-152.

Huber, G., & Lewis, K. (2010). Cross-Understanding: Implications for group cognition and performance. *Academy of Management Review, 35* (1), 6-26.

Hudson, F. (1999). *The handbook of coaching: A comprehensive resource guide for managers, executives, consultants, and human resource professionals.* San Francisco, CA: Jossey-Bass.

Hunter, D. (2007). *The art of facilitation.* San Francisco, CA: Jossey-Bass.

Iacono, C.S. & Weisband, S. (1997). *Developing trust in virtual teams.* Presented at the 30th International Conference of System Sciences, Maui, HI, January.

Janis, I.L. (1983). Groupthink. In H.H. Blumberg, A.P. Hare, V. Kent, & M.F. Davis (Eds.), *Small groups and social interaction* (Vol. 2, pp. 39-46). New York, NY: Wiley.

Jarvenpaa, S.L., Knoll, K., & Leidner, D., (1998). Is anybody out there?: The implications of trust in global virtual teams. *Journal of Management Information Systems,* 14, 29-64.

Jacobs, M. & Goodman, G. (1989). Psychology and self-help groups: Prediction on a partnership. *American Psychologist, 44,* 536-545.

Jones, C. (1998). Evaluating a collaborative online learning environment. *Active Learning,* No 9.

Jones, S. (1998). Cybersociety 2.0. Thousands Oaks: Sage Publications.

Joyce, B. and Showers, B. (1996). The Evolution of peer coaching.
Educational Leadership, 53 (6): 12–16.

Judge, W. & Cowell, J. (1997). The brave new world of executive coaching. *Business Horizons, 40(4), 71-77.*

Kampa-Kokesch, S., & Anderson, M., (2001). Executive coach: A comprehensive review of the literature.

Consulting Psychology Journal: Research and Practice, 53(4), 205-228.

Kaplan, R. (1979). The conspicuous absence of evidence that process consultation enhances task performance. *Journal of Applied Behavioral Science, 15,* 346-360.

Kaplan, R. (1991). *Beyond ambition. How driven managers can lead better and live better.* San Francisco, CA: Jossey-Bass Publishers.

Kaufmann, C. & Bachkirova, T. (2009). Spinning order from chaos: How do we know *what* to study in coaching research and is it for self-reflective practice? In S. Palmer (Ed.), *Coaching: An International Journal of Theory, Research and Practice, 2*(1).

Kegan, R. (1982). *The Evolving Self.* Cambridge, MA: Harvard University Press.

Kegan, R. (1994). *In over our heads: The mental demands of modern life.* Cambridge, MA: Harvard University Press.

Kets de Vries, M. (1991). *Organizations on the couch.* San Francisco, CA: Jossey-Bass.

Kets de Vries, M. (2005). Leadership group coaching in action: Zen of creating high performance teams. *Academy of Management Executive, 19 (1).*

Kilburg, R. (1996). Executive coaching as an emerging competency in the practice of consultation. *Consultation Psychology Journal: Practice and Research, 48*, 59-60.

Kilburg, R. (2007). Introduction: The historical and conceptual roots of executive coaching. In R. R. Kilburg & R. C. Diedrich (Eds.), *The wisdom of coaching* (pp. 3-15). Washington, DC.: American Psychological Association.

Kolbe, R.H. & Burnett, M.S. (1991). Content-analysis research: An examination of applications with directives for improving research reliability and objectivity. *Journal of Consumer Research, 18*, 243-250.

Kozlowski, S. W. J., & Bell, B. S. (2003). Work groups and teams in organizations. In W. C. Borman,D. R. Ilgen, & R. J. Klimoski (Eds.), *Handbook of psychology (Vol. 12): Industrial*

and Organizational Psychology (pp. 333-375). New York, NY: Wiley.

Knowles, M. (1990). *The adult learner: A neglected species (4th ed.)*. Houston, TX: Gulf.

KPMG. (2008). *International Coach Federation Global Coaching Study, Executive Summary*. Rev. 2008. KPMG, 2007, p. 2.

Krugman, P. (1991). Myths and realities of U.S. competitiveness. *Science, 254,* 811-815.

Kress, D. (2008). A phenomenological study exploring executive coaching: understanding perceptions of self awareness and leadership behavior changes. *Dissertation Abstracts International* (UMI No. 3324089).

LeBon, G. (1895). *The crowd.* London: England: Ernest Benn.

Leonard, T. (1988). *The portable coach.* New York, NY: Scribner.

Levine, J. & Moreland, R. (1990). Progress in small group research. *Annual Review of Psychology, 41,* 585-634.

Lewin, K., retrieved online at (http://www.psychology.sbc.edu/Kurt%20Lewin.htm) on March 13, 2009.

Lewin, K. (1945). *Resolving social conflicts: Selected papers on group dynamics.* New York, NY: Harper & Brothers.

Lewin, K. (1947). *Group decision and social change,* In T.M. Newcomb, & E.L. Hartley, (Eds.,), *Readings in social psychology, p. 344..* New York, NY: Henry Holt & Co., p. 344.

Lewin, K. (1951). *Field theory in social science.* New York: Harper.

Lieberman, M. (1994). Growth groups in the 1980s: Mental health implications. In A. Fuhriman & G.M. Burlingame (Eds.), *Handbook of group psychotherapy: An empirical and clinical synthesis* (pp. 527-558). New York, NY: Wiley.

Lipnack, J. & Stamps, J. (1997). *Virtual teams.* New York: John Wiley & Sons, Inc.

Lipnack, J., & Stamps, J. (2010). *Leading virtual teams.* Boston, MA: Harvard Business School.

Machan, D., (1988, June). Sigmund Freud meets Henry Ford. *Forbes.* pp. 1-2.

Majchrzak, A., Malhotra, A., Stamps, J., & Lipnack, J. (2004, May). Can absence make a team grow stronger? *Harvard Business Review: Best Practice,* pp. 131-137.

Maslow, A. H. (1968). *Toward a psychology of being,* (2nd ed.) Princeton, NJ: D. Van Nostrand Company Inc.

Mayer, R.C., Davis, J.H., & Schoorman, F.D. (1995). An integrative model of organizational trust. *Academy of Management Review, 20,* (3), 709-734.

McCall, M. (1998). *High flyers.* Boston, MA: Harvard Business School Press.

McGrath, J.E. (1984). *Groups: Interaction and performance.* Englewood Cliffs, NJ: Prentice-Hall.

Mc Grath, J., & Argote, L. (2003). Group processes in organizational contexts. In M. Hogg & S. Tindale, (Eds.,) *Blackwell handbook of social psychology: Group processes* (pp. 603-627).

Malden, MA: Blackwell.

McLaughlin, B., & Oksenberg, R., (Eds). (1988). *Perspectives on self-deception.* London: University of California Press.

McLean, G. (1997). Multi-rater 360 feedback. In L. J. Bassi & D. Russ-Eft (Eds.), *What works: Assessment, development, and measurement* (pp. 87-108). Alexandria, VA: American Society for Training and Development.

Merriam, S., Caffarella, R., & Baumgartner, L., (2007). *Learning in adulthood: A comprehensive guide, (3rd ed.)* San Francisco, CA: John Wiley & Sons.

Moreland, R., Hogg, M., & Haines, S. (1994). Back to the future: Social psychological research on groups. *Journal of Experimental Social Psychology, 30,* 527-555.

Mullen, B. & Copper, C. (1994). The relation between group cohesiveness and performance: An integration. *Psychological Bulletin, 115* (2), 210-227.

Natale, S., & Diamante, T. (2005). The five stages of executive coaching: Better process makes better practice. *Journal of Business Ethics,* 59(4), 361-374.

Neuendorf, K. (2002). *The Content analysis guidebook.* Thousand Oaks, CA: Sage.

Neuman, L.W. (2003). *Social research methods. Qualitative and quantitative approaches,* (5th ed). Boston, MA: Pearson Education.

O'Hefferman, P.O. (1986, April). The Silicon Valley's successful coach. *Santa Clara County Business, 4,* 23.

O'Neill, M. (2000). *Executive coaching with backbone and heart: A systems approach to engaging leaders with their challenges.* San Francisco, CA: Jossey-Bass.

Page, L. (2003). Adler and the profession of coaching. *The Journal of Individual Psychology,* 59 (1), 86-93.

Patwell, B. & Seashore, E.W. (2006). *Triple impact coaching: Use-of-Self in the coaching process.* Columbia, MD: Bingham House Books.

Pepitone, A. (1981). Lessons from the history of social psychology. *American Psychologist, 36* (9), 972-985.

Peterson, D.B. (1996). Executive coaching at work: The art of one-on-one change. *Consulting Psychology Journal: Practice and Research, 48,* 78-86.

Poole, M., & Hollingshead, A. (2005). *Theories of small groups: Interdisciplinary perspectives.* Thousand Oaks, CA: Sage Publications.

Polster, E., & Polster, M. (1973). *Gestalt therapy integrated: Contours of theory and practice.* New York, NY: Vintage Books.

Posthuma, B. (1999). *Small groups in counseling and therapy: Process and leadership.* Boston, MA: Allyn & Bacon.

Rheingold, H. (1993). *The virtual community.* Boston, MA: Addison Wesley Press.

Rogers, C. R. & Dymond, R. F. (eds.) Psychotherapy and Personality Change. Chapter 15, The Case of Mrs. Oak, pp.259-348. Chicago: University of Chicago Press.

Rosenbaum, M., & Berger, M. (1975). *Group psychotherapy and group function (rev. ed.).* New York, NY: Basic Books.

Rossman, B. (1993). Group cohesion: Intergroup and intragroup relations. *Dissertation Abstracts International,* UMI, 9409450.

Schwartz, R. (2002). *The skilled facilitator: A comprehensive resource for consultants, facilitators, managers, trainers, and coaches.* San Francisco, CA: Jossey-Bass.

Seashore, C.N., Seashore, E.W., & Weinberg, G.M. (1992). *What did you say? The art of giving and receiving feedback.* Columbia, MD: Bingham Books.

Sherman, S. & Freas, A., (2004, November). The wild west of executive coaching. *Harvard Business Review, Nov 2004.*

Short, S., & Short, M. (2005). Essay: Role of the coach in the coach-athlete relationship. *Lancet, 366,* S20-S30.

Showers, B., Murphy, C., & Joyce, B. (1996). The River City program: Staff development becomes school improvement. In B. Joyce and E. Calhoun (Eds.), *Learning experiences in school renewal: An exploration of five successful programs* (pp. 13–51). Eugene, OR: ERIC Clearinghouse on Educational Management.

Silsbee, D. (2004). *The mindful coach, Seven roles for helping people grow.* Marshall, NC: Ivy River Press.

Silverman, D. (2006). *Interpreting qualitative data: Methods for analyzing talk, text and interactions, 3rd ed.* Los Angeles, CA: Sage Publications.

Skiffington, S., & Zeus, P. (2008). *Behavioral coaching: How to build sustainable personal and organizational strength.* New York, NY: McGraw-Hill Companies.

Snow, C.C., Snell, S.A., & Davison, S.C. (1996). Use transactional teams to globalize your company. *Organizational Dynamics, 24*, (4), 50-67.

Stein, I. (2003), Introduction: Beginning a promising conversion. In I. F. Stein & L. A. Belsten (Eds.), *Proceedings of the first ICF coaching research symposium November 12, 2003 Denver, Colorado USA* (pp. vii-xii). Mooresville, NC: Paw Print Press.

Steiner, I. (1974). Whatever happened to the group in social psychology? *Journal of Experimental Social Psychology, 10,* 94-108.

Stern, L. (2004a). Executive coaching: A working definition. *Consulting Psychology Journal: Research and Practice, 56(3), 154-162.*

Stern, L. (2004b). *The executive coaching handbook: Principles and guidelines for a successful coaching partnership, (3rd ed.).* Developed for The Executive Coaching Forum, www.executivecoachingforum.com.

Stober, D.R. (2005). Approaches to research on executive and organizational coaching outcomes. *International Journal of Coaching in Organizations, 3*(1), 6-13.

Stober, D. R. (2006). Coaching from the humanistic perspective. In D. R. Stober & A. M.

Grant (Eds.), *Evidence based coaching handbook: Putting best practices to work*
for your clients (pp. 17–50). Hoboken, NJ: John Wiley & Sons.

Stober, D. & Grant, A. (Eds.). (2006). *Evidenced based coaching handbook: Putting best practices to work for your clients.* New Jersey: John Wiley & Sons.

Stone, A. (1991). Will the real body please stand up? Boundary stories about virtual cultures. In M. Benedikt (Ed.), *Cyberspace* (pp. 81-118). Cambridge: MIT Press.

Sztucinski, K. (2001). The nature of executive coaching: An exploration of the executive's experience. *Dissertation Abstracts International, 62* (10, 4826B. UMI No. 3029593).

Thibaut, J., & Kelley, H. (1959). *The social psychology of groups.* New York, NY: John Wiley & Sons.

Thomas, K., & Velthouse, B. (1990). Cognitive elements of empowerment: An interpretive model of intrinsic task motivation. *Academy of management review,* 15: 666-681.

Thorn, A., McLeod, M., & Goldsmith, M. (2007). *Peer coaching overview.* Unpublished manuscript.

Thornton, C. (2010). *Group and team coaching: The essential guide.* London, UK: Routledge: Taylor and Francis Group.

Tobias, L. (1996). Coaching executives. *Consulting Psychology Journal: Practice and Research, 48,* 87-95.

Vilas, S. (2003). *Becoming a coach: The Coachinc.com approach.* Steamboat Springs: Coach U Press.

Waclawski, J., & Church, A. (1999a). A feedback-based model of executive coaching. Presentation delivered at the annual meeting of the National Academy of Management, August 8-11, Chicago.

Waclawski, J., & Church, A. (1999b, Summer). Four easy steps to performance coaching. *Performance in Practice,* pp. 4-5.

Walther, J.B., Bunz, U., & Bazarova, N.N. (2005, August). *The rules of virtual groups.* Paper presented at the International Conference on System Sciences, Hawaii.

Watson, G. (1928). Do groups think more efficiently than individuals? *The Journal of Abnormal and Social Psychology,* 23 (3), 328-336.

Weiss, R.S. (1994). *Learning from strangers: The Art and method of qualitative interview studies.* New York, NY: The Free Press.

Weller, D., & Weller, K. (2004). Coaching and performance: Substantiating the link. *Leadership in Action*, 24(2), 20-21.

Whitmore, J. (1992) *Coaching for performance. (1ˢᵗ Edition).* London, UK: Nicholas Brealey.

Whitworth, L., Kimsey-House, H., & Sandahl, P., (1998). *Co-active coaching*. Palo Alto, CA: Davies-Black.

Whitmore, J. (2003) *Coaching for performance. Growing people, performance and purpose (3ʳᵈ Edition).* London, UK: Nicholas Brealey.

Williams, J.L. (1995). What makes a profession a profession? *Professional Safety, 43*(1), 18.

Yalom, I. (1975). *The theory and practice of group psychotherapy (2ⁿᵈ ed.).* New York, NY: Basic Books.

Yalom, I. & Leszcz, M. (2005). *The theory and practice of group psychotherapy (5ᵗʰ ed.).* New York, NY: Basic Books, Inc., Publishers.

Zofi, Y. (2012). *A manager's guide to virtual teams.* New York, NY: American Management Association Press.

Appendix A

INTERVIEW PROTOCOL
DECEMBER 2010 – REVISED VERSION
Approved by Institutional Review Board

RESEARCH QUESTION:

What are the experiences of business professionals who participate in a group coaching process virtually?

Opening Remarks to respondent: Thank you for agreeing to speak with me today and taking the time to share your experiences with your group coaching process. Let's begin with you sharing about your experience in the group coaching process.

1. What were the dates of your group coaching experience?

2. Can you please tell me about how you chose to enter into this *group* coaching process?

3. Tell me generally about this virtual group coaching process experience? How was it conducted? How long did the sessions last? What topics were usually discussed?

4. Did you learn anything about yourself in this group coaching process?

5. Did you learn anything about group coaching in particular?

6. Tell me about the virtual part of your experience. To what degree did being virtual influence your interactions with the other individuals involved?

7. Did you ever get to the point where you felt you could share openly about important issues?

8. If so, how long did the call(s) go on before you felt that way and was there anything that was said or done by the coach or other members of the group that facilitated that openness?

9. What words would you use to describe what it was like to be a participant in this group coaching process?

10. Were there times when you felt uncomfortable being in the "group process?"
What caused these uncomfortable feelings?

11. What do you see as being positive aspects about your experience participating in this virtual group coaching process?

12. What do you see as being negative aspects of your virtual group coaching experience?

13. Do you see any *advantages* of the group coaching being virtual versus being face to face?

14. Do you see any *disadvantages* of being virtual versus in this group coaching process versus in a one-on-one coaching process?

15. Is there anything else about your group coaching experience that you would like to share?

16. Please tell me about yourself.

    a. Age Range:

        18 – 25   26 – 35   36 – 45   46 – 60

    b. Ethnicity:_____

    c. Highest education level: _____

    d. Occupation: _____

    e. What was/is your prior coaching experience?

        _____

        _____

        _____

    f. How many months were you involved in this group coaching process?_____

    g. Would you participate in another group coaching process?_____

17. Are you aware of anyone else who has participated in a group coaching process that would be willing to participate in my study? I am trying to contact as many people as possible to strengthen my research.

18. Once I have analyzed the data, I would like to share the results with those who have participated in the research. I plan to do this on a conference call. If you

are interested, I will contact you and see if you are interested and available to hear what I have found and discuss the results with the others who have participated. Would this be acceptable to you?

www.ingramcontent.com/pod-product-compliance
Lightning Source LLC
Chambersburg PA
CBHW050129280326
41933CB00010B/1302